DO PARTIES MAKE A DIFFERENCE?

CHATHAM HOUSE SERIES ON CHANGE IN AMERICAN POLITICS
Edited by Aaron Wildavsky
University of California, Berkeley

Also by Richard Rose

United Kingdom Facts, with Ian McAllister
Can Government Go Bankrupt? with Guy Peters
What Is Governing? Purpose and Policy in Washington
Managing Presidential Objectives
Northern Ireland: A Time of Choice
The Problem of Party Government
International Almanac of Electoral History, with T. T. Mackie
Governing without Consensus
People in Politics
Influencing Voters
Politics in England
Must Labour Lose? with Mark Abrams
The British General Election of 1959, with D. E. Butler

Edited by Richard Rose

Presidents and Prime Ministers, with Ezra Suleiman
Electoral Participation
Britain: Progress and Decline, with William B. Gwyn
Challenge to Governance
Elections without Choice, with Guy Hermet and Alain Rouquié
New Trends in British Politics, with Dennis Kavanagh
The Dynamics of Public Policy
Comparing Public Policies with Jerzy Wiatr
The Management of Urban Change in Britain and Germany
Electoral Behavior: A Comparative Handbook
Lessons from America
European Politics, with Mattei Dogan
Policy-Making in Britain
Studies in British Politics

DO PARTIES MAKE A DIFFERENCE?

Richard Rose
Centre for the Study of Public Policy
University of Strathclyde

CHATHAM HOUSE PUBLISHERS, INC.
Chatham, New Jersey

DO PARTIES MAKE A DIFFERENCE?

CHATHAM HOUSE PUBLISHERS, INC.
Box One, Chatham, New Jersey 07928

Publisher: Edward Artinian
Design: Quentin Fiore
Composition: Columbia Publishing Company, Inc.
Printing and Binding: Hamilton Printing Company

Library of Congress Cataloging in Publication Data
Rose, Richard, 1933–
    Do parties make a difference?

    (Chatham House series on change in American politics)
    Includes bibliographical references and index.
    1. Political parties—Great Britain. 2. Elections
—Great Britain. 3. Great Britain—Politics and govern-
ment—1945—   I. Title.   II. Series.
JN1121.R667   324.241   80-15818
ISBN 0-934540-08-X

Manufactured in the United States of America
10 9 8 7 6 5 4 3 2 1

To ROSEMARY *who certainly makes a difference*

Contents

List of Tables

List of Figures

Acknowledgments

This study concentrates on what parties do in office. Does the record of a Conservative government differ significantly from that of a Labour government? In many respects, this book is thus a sequel to *The Problem of Party Government*, in which I analyzed how parties compete at elections and act as organizations, and the problems politicians face on entering the dark corridors of government office.

The immediate stimulus to write this book came from Italy, where the advent of Fascism in 1922 demonstrated to Italians that there is a big difference between some parties. Since then Italians have speculated, at times optimistically and at times apprehensively, about how much difference can result from a change of party control of government. Today, the only alternative to the long-reigning Christian Democrats are the Communists. Following the ambiguous *compromeso storico* between Christian Democrats and Communists, the Agnelli Foundation of Turin decided to commission studies of the influence of party government in major European societies. A paper written for that project led me to examine the question more fully, and this book is the result.

In writing about party government in Britain, I have been able to draw upon firsthand knowledge acquired over a quarter-century of research in British party politics. But in no sense is this book a personal recollection or an inside dopester's account of what high-ranking politicians thought they were doing. As the chapters demonstrate, selective and subjective observations can often be misleading. The conclusions of this book are based upon a rigorous and systematic sifting of the evidence of *what government (and opposition) actually did*. The book is short because it concentrates on the forest rather than particular trees.

The compilation of many of the tables herein was untertaken by Richard Parry of the Centre for the Study of Public Policy, who worked with the meticulousness of an ex-civil servant and the intellectual concerns of a promising scholar. Data from unpublished as well as published annual surveys of parliamentary legislation were made available by Ivor F. Burton and Gavin Drewry of Bedford College, University of London, whose work merits the careful scrutiny of persons interested in contemporary parliamentary affairs. Unpublished as well as published data from public opinion surveys have been made available by the Gallup poll and National Opinion polls. Useful comments on portions of the work in progress were received from Dennis Kavanagh of Manchester University, Philip Norton of Hull University, and Malcolm Punnett of Strathclyde as well as from practising politicians. Mrs. R. West, with assistance from colleagues, has once again produced the necessary typescripts of a book with both speed and accuracy.

In case an inquisitive reader might wish to know something about my own political party bias, it is outside the main alignments of the British party system, being that of a border-state Truman Democrat. The experience of studying party politics in Britain through the years has generated a liking for the people involved, and a respect for the system they operate. But it has also produced too much evidence of things gone awry for me to commit myself to any party. My personal concern is more with the issues of British politics than the parties that deal with them, and this is probably the view of the majority of the British electorate today.

RICHARD ROSE
Bennochy
Helensburgh

DO PARTIES MAKE A DIFFERENCE?

Why look at a crystal ball when you can read the bloody book?
ANEURIN BEVAN

Introduction

British government is party government—but that does not ensure that it is good government. The conventional view of Westminster democracy has taken for granted that party government was both necessary and desirable. Only by placing all the powers of government in the hands of a single party could a country be effectively governed by politicians strong enough to take unpopular but necessary decisions. Only by offering the electorate a choice between the record of the party in office and the criticism of the opposition could the electorate effectively hold politicians accountable.[1]

British politicians have long assumed that parties can and should make a difference in the way that the country is governed. The belief has tended to intensify, the greater the problems facing the country. In the 1930s, the Conservative and Labour parties often appeared as if they represented more or less mutually exclusive ideologies, with very different prescriptions for resolving the country's difficulties. With the recurrence of economic difficulties in the 1960s and 1970s, the language has been heard again. Edward Heath said of the 1970 Conservative election victory: "We were returned to office to change the course and the history of this nation, nothing else." The February 1974 Labour Party manifesto declared an intention to bring about a fundamental and irreversible shift in the balance of power and wealth—albeit a shift in the opposite direction from that proposed by the Conservative government.[2]

The 1974 general election result was a signal that a significant portion of the electorate no longer trusted either major party to govern Britain. In case politicians did not get the message in February, it was repeated in October, when one-quarter of the vote was cast for representatives of "third force" parties, principally the Liberals. Even though three-quarters of the voters still endorsed the idea of either a Labour or a Conservative government, many commentators jumped to the conclusion that party government had "failed."

In the introduction to a serious academic study of electoral reform, the Gladstone Professor of Government at Oxford, S. E. Finer, argued that the adversary system of party government in Britain had become bad government. Giving unqualified power first to one party and then another made government policy swing from one extreme to another, and the uncertainties generated in anticipation of every general election were bad for the country and bad for government. Finer recommended adopting proportional representation in order to create a coalition government at Westminster to correct the abuses diagnosed. In 1977, *The Economist* went further, rejecting the conventional model of British party government in an apparently serious five-page Guy Fawkes Day article entitled "Blowing Up a Tyranny."[3]

The criticisms of the existing party system must be taken seriously when they are heard from its beneficiaries. As ex-Cabinet ministers have grown older, they have grown more radical, being prepared to endorse all kinds of constraints on party government that they had not canvassed when initially seeking office.[4] For example, Roy Jenkins, after twenty-eight years in the House of Commons and nine as a minister, has concluded that there is need for a radical change from the "constricting rigidity—almost the tyranny—of the present party system." Notwithstanding a lifetime of activity in the Labour Party, Jenkins has attacked "the tyranny of the belief, against all the evidence, that one government can make or break us." The former Chancellor of the Exchequer confessed to having contributed to this belief.

> New governments became more and more enthusiastic in promising the one thing they could not deliver: a higher rate of economic growth.... but not in a mood of questioning humility. The opposition party of the day always believed it had the philosopher's stone.
>
> Elect us, they—including me—said, and the economy will bound forward. Quite often they were elected, but the economy did nothing of the sort. The result was a widening gap between promise and performance.[5]

Both professorial and politician critics agree that parties do make a difference to the way in which Britain is governed. But this only makes matters worse. Jenkins has charged, "Most of these changes exacerbate rather than cure the fundamental economic ill, and irritate rather than satisfy the mass of the electorate."[6]

The 1979 general election indicated that four-fifths of the voters do not agree with the critics. The Conservatives were returned with a clear-cut parliamentary majority, as the pendulum familiarly swung against a

Labour government whose record in difficult international circumstances had made it vulnerable to opposition criticism. Moreover, the Liberals, who had acted as a "brake" on conventional party government in 1977–78, saw their vote go down.

In the 1979 election campaign, all the parties testified to their belief that the outcome should make a big difference to the country's government. In a foreword to the Conservative manifesto, Margaret Thatcher wrote of an allegedly growing "threat to freedom" and "a feeling of helplessness" generated by Labour rule. She warned, "This election may be the last chance to reverse that process." The manifesto declared, "Our country's relative decline is not inevitable. We in the Conservative Party think we can reverse it."[7]

Notwithstanding left-wing criticisms that it did not go far enough, the 1979 Labour manifesto also proclaimed great differences between "the Tory programme of confrontation and social injustice" and what it described as Labour's policy of offering "cooperation in place of confrontation; instead of division, social justice." Labour warned against the election of a Conservative government: "Too much is at stake to let the Conservatives frustrate the hopes of the coming decade by turning back the clock."

Even the Liberals paid a backhanded tribute to the power if not the performance of the present system of party government by denouncing alternative Conservative and Labour governments for causing a political "deadlock that has meant economic and social decline." The 1979 Liberal manifesto described the election as offering a big difference, "a chance to change a failed political system" by voting for a coalition government in which the Liberals would play a prominent part.

The Parliament elected to govern Britain until 1984 contains 635 MPs committed to the belief that parties make a difference. The fact that MPs think party politics makes a difference is not proof of this assertion. The cynic might answer: They would. Whether the Conservative or Labour Party is in office makes a difference to the jobs and status of hundreds of MPs, and the morale of thousands of party activists. However, it does not follow that the 13 million who voted for the winner—or the even larger number who did not—will notice a difference as well.

But *can* parties make a difference? The average politician is likely to believe the answer is yes, and a political leader is even more likely to believe that by an act of will great changes can be made in national affairs. Faith in the "great man" theory of history dies hard—especially among those who see themselves called to play that role. Margaret Thatcher, perhaps because she is a successful woman among men, is no exception to this rule. In the 1979 election campaign, she rejected the idea that a party's task should be to manage a country's affairs so equably that it left little distinctive imprint upon the nation. At Cardiff on 16 April she declared:

> I am a conviction politician. The Old Testament prophets did not say "Brothers, I want a consensus." They said: "This is my faith. This is what I passionately believe. If you believe it too, then come with me."

Immediately after the election, however, voters showed that they did not wish to follow her with blind conviction. From the first Gallup poll after the election, the Conservatives have consistently trailed the Labour Party.

The installation of a new Prime Minister, a new Cabinet and an exchange of place between the Conservative and Labour parties in the House of Commons does not ipso facto dispose of all the difficulties of governing a country. Many things that influence the condition of the people are not altered by a game of musical chairs in Downing Street. Trade unions, banks, industrialists and professional associations represent permanent and powerful interests in society. The economic weaknesses that frustrate one government remain to frustrate its successor too. And the constraints of the international economy are even less immediately influenced by domestic political events.

If an act of will could deal with Britain's recurring problems, then one or another resident of Downing Street would have done so long ago. If the electorate could collectively will a government that would produce peace and prosperity, it too would have discovered this long ago. Unfortunately, the government of Britain is not so easily put to rights. This can be a source of reassurance not despair, Peregrine Worsthorne argued, immediately before the 1979 general election:

> It is important to emphasise the reality of British politics: the true nature of elections. They are not *coups d'etat*. Even if Mrs. Thatcher were some demented Ayatollah, anxious to pull everything up by the roots, which of course she is not, the mere fact of winning an election would not allow her to give vent to her alleged passions.
>
> The balance of power in British society does not suddenly change because a new face appears in Downing Street. If the trade unions are strong now, so they will remain, whatever happens on May 3.
>
> At best Mrs. Thatcher will be able to edge the country slightly rightward. If she makes a mess of this attempt, there will be opportunity soon enough for the electorate to have second thoughts. Nothing irrevo-

cable will take place this week. That is not how British democracy works. [8]

Yet if parties do make some difference to the way that Britain is governed, and even Worsthorne concedes that, what kind of difference is it? The difference may be measured quantitatively, by assessing changes in the rate of economic growth under parties nominally committed to Socialist and free market policies, or changes in the number of owner-occupier or council houses built under parties committed to different housing policies.

The most important differences between parties may be intangible changes in the national mood, induced by the style of a particular Prime Minister or the general image of the party in office. For example, unions may feel more confidence in a Labour government, and business more confidence in a Conservative government, irrespective of their actual performance in office. Middle-class people may relax in the belief that power is in the hands of the "right" set of people if there is a Conservative government, and working-class Britons identify more happily with authority if the country is governed by those they believe understand best how ordinary people live.

Sometimes, differences and discontinuities in policy occur within the life of a government, rather than between governments. Both Conservative and Labour governments have shown themselves adept at steering policy in a graceful arc that, in the fullness of time, looks suspiciously like a U-turn to its critics. One expert on incomes policy has counted five different policies of the 1964–70 Labour government; five different policies of the 1970–74 Conservative government, and six different policies of the 1974–79 Labour government. [9] Within the lifetime of a single Parliament, each party in power has tried variations on two opposing themes — conciliation and coercion.

How much difference do we want a change in government to make? The electoral system normally produces a winner-take-all result. Either the Conservative or Labour Party secures 100 percent of the power in government. But at every election since 1945, no party has won as much as 50 percent of the popular vote. Every government since then has seen more people vote against it than for it. In 1979, five voters rejected the Conservative Party for every four that cast a vote for it. When the government of the day lacks full endorsement by the electorate, then whatever direction it proceeds, there is a case for it to move as if with the handbrake on.

The purpose of this book is to test *whether* parties make a difference in the way in which Britain is governed, and if so, what difference? To do this, there is no need to gaze into a crystal ball. The record of successive Conservative and Labour governments is in full view, and it is wise to follow Aneurin Bevan's suggestion that it should be read.

The chapters that follow concentrate attention upon the public actions of parties and governments. What government does cannot be hidden for long from the British people. The public evidence of what government does is more important than the private discussions of politicians making policies, or the highly subjective ruminations of Cabinet ministers after the event, whether confided to a diary or to a David Frost. If government's policies are to have an impact on society, they must become a matter of public record. There is no such thing as a "secret" policy with "secret" consequences, in peacetime at least. *Hansard* contains many monuments of a government's achievements and of things left undone. The consequences of government actions are revealed in the publications of the Treasury, the Central Statistical Office and the International Monetary Fund as well. They are also evident in the everyday experience of the electorate, who must cope with the effects of what government does. One of the burdens of the Conservative and Labour parties today is that their record in office may be too familiar to the electorate.

The British party system has often been admired as an ideal for representative government, abroad as well as at home. Americans wishing for a clearer and more effective choice at elections have particularly praised party government in Britain. There are at least three major reasons why examining how parties work in Britain provides an appropriate test of the workings of representative government.

First, the results of a general election have normally fixed responsibility for governing in the hands of a single party. Because of the fusion of executive, legislative and party leadership in the same hands, the party winning a British general election gains authority over all of government. This authority is not checked by judicial review or the constraints of federalism. By contrast, in America the winner of a presidential election does not enjoy authority over Congress, the Supreme Court or other levels of government in the federal system. In Scandinavia, Belgium, the Netherlands, Italy and other parts of Europe, control of government is normally vested in a coalition of parties, thus blurring responsibility among several parties in government.

A second reason why British experience is specially useful to test the impact of parties is that the Conservative and Labour parties have normally alternated in office from 1945 to 1979. Each party has been in office for seventeen years. In America, even though a Republican has held the White House for sixteen of the thirty-five years from 1945 to 1980, during that period the Democrats have almost always been a majority in Congress. Moreover, the circumstances in which John F. Kennedy, Lyndon Johnson and Richard Nixon each left office are not thought to exemplify the normal practice of American politics. At the other extreme, in Sweden the Social Democrats were in power for more than forty years up to 1976, and the Fifth French Republic, founded in 1958, has yet to see the Presidency pass from centre-right to left-wing hands.

Third, the Conservative and Labour parties are familiar examples of parties found in nearly every Western nation. Labour is a party that recurringly faces the dilemma of reconciling a relatively timeless Socialist (some would argue, Marxist) ideology with the pragmatic demands of winning elections and governing with "moderate" or social democratic policies. The Conservatives are a "catchall" party, seeking support where it can be found and normally avoiding any clear statement of ideology except the ideology of electoral success. As long as both parties give first priority to electoral victory, the differences between them are likely to be limited. By contrast, Italians have regarded the difference between Christian Democrats and Communists as too great to risk the experiment of coalition government, let alone the alternation of parties in office.

The conditions that make British party government distinctive are rooted in the history and institutions of the country. The consequences of this distinctiveness are less often considered. Comparisons with other nations can be helpful to underline them. For example, the disciplined advance of programmatic aims by British parties stands in marked contrast to the position that a newly elected American President faces, when he looks at Congress and realizes that his principal enemies are within government, not outside it. Yet the very incoherence of American parties makes them open to new ideas and new groups, and ready to respond to change by assimilating them.

Clearly stated concepts are necessary to identify the evidence needed to test the record of party government, and to determine in what ways, if any, parties make a difference. Chapter 1 defines the terms of reference of this study and the ideas that constitute the basic assumptions of the familiar model of party government. Chapter 2 shows that when the idea of party government is analyzed rigorously, it may refer to any of four different models, two Adversary models, and two Consensus models. The models are tested in five subsequent chapters. The views of the electorate are examined first, since it is the voters that parties are meant to represent. The next chapter considers to what extent parties apply their manifestos when in office, or whether a persisting difference in British politics is between the intentions of manifestos and government practice. The behaviour of adversaries in Parliament is examined in chapter 5, and the extent to which parties seek to reorganize the institutions of government to their own advantage in chapter 6. The management of the economy — the chief concern of every party for decades — is assessed next in terms of the inputs of government policy and outcomes in the economy. The concluding chapter gives a straightforward reply to the book's title: *Do Parties Make a Difference?*

CHAPTER I

Parties and Public Policy

Elections are about what people want — but people cannot always have what they want. The British electoral system effectively makes voters the prisoners of parties. The electorate is offered a choice between voting for a Conservative or Labour government, or voting in protest against both. Parties name the leaders, define issues and adopt the programme alternatives between which voters must choose. The organization of parties gives meaning to the otherwise inarticulate and unorganized views of individuals. By their votes electors effectively empower a party to carry into practice what it has talked about in the election campaign, and then some. It is the party victorious in an election and not public opinion that has the immediate authority to decide and implement policies.

The policies that a party enunciates are best described as political intentions. In the absence of positive accomplishments they are not to be treated as achievements. Intentions identify what a party would like the government to do about problems facing the country. It is sometimes argued that the policy intentions of politicians are so much "campaign oratory," empty phrases that no one (least of all the politician voicing them) expects to take seriously. Yet if this be so, it still leaves a question: Why are they proclaimed? If a party's policy intentions are meant to be misleading, who is fooled: the politicians who formulate them, or the electorate?

A party can try to carry out its policy intentions only if it is in government. In opposition, a party has neither the right nor the power to determine what government does. In office, a party enjoys the legitimate authority of government. It may start by repeating its policy intentions voiced in opposition. But it must do more than that. It must also try to put its intentions into practice. The actions it takes to carry out its intentions, along with reactions to unanticipated events, constitute the record of what a party does in practice.

Government is about what people can have. Invariably there is a gap between the intentions that a party enunciates in an election campaign and what it achieves in practice. In preparing an election manifesto, especially if in opposition, a party can engage in "superman" planning, proposing to leap barriers that no previous government has overcome, and shape society as it wishes. In the course of an election campaign, a party can even promise to do what may be impossible, as long as the promise does not damage its credibility with the electorate.

Many theories of party government confuse intentions and accomplishments.[1] The first section of this chapter states carefully the assumptions that must be made if parties are expected to make policy in government.[2] This is followed by a review of party government in Britain in the past generation, the period in which this book is set.

The Basic Assumptions

Parties are necessary and important in determining who governs, but it does not follow that they are equally important in determining what government does. For this to be the case, four basic assumptions must each be true. A moment's reflection will show that none of these assumptions can be taken for granted. While each is familiar and plausible, there are also good reasons for assuming its exact opposite.

First, to assume that parties have policy intentions is to go beyond the minimalist conception of a party. The only attributes necessary by definition are that a party nominates candidates and contests elections. A general election can be reduced to a popularity contest between competing political personalities, or a vote of confidence (or no confidence) in the relative competence of alternative teams of politicians. Even if a party does not have any policies, the government it seeks to lead does. To deny parties any role in making government policy invites the question: Who does make policy, if not the party elected to do so?[3]

American writers often endorse the minimalist definition of party politics without policies.[4] In doing this, American political scientists reflect a cultural bias, for American parties are notoriously *un*programmatic. The sole national election—the presidential race—is a contest between individuals. Issues can be important, but they are not so much related to differences between American parties as between candidates, including candidates of the same party pitted against each other in primary elections. To view parties solely as individuals or teams competing for electoral victory is to deny any further purpose to parties. An election victory would be an end in itself, like victory in a boxing or football match, and not a means to larger political ends.

Continental European writers, by contrast, normally assume that parties have larger political purposes as well. This is most evident among writers who postulate that there are mutually exclusive "grand designs" or ideologies in society (e.g., Catholicism and Communism) and that electorally oriented parties *ought to and do* reflect these different outlooks in policies affecting the totality of social life.

In Britain there are differing emphases upon the place of policy in party politics. *The Problem of Party Government* devotes more than a third of its length to the policy concerns of parties. By contrast, Robert T. McKenzie's well-known study of *British Political Parties* excludes policy concerns in its opening sentences.[5] The Marxist author Ralph Miliband argues in *Parliamentary Socialism* that the Labour Party ought to have a radical, even revolutionary set of policies — and then claims to explain why it is not a "truly" Socialist party.[6] Conservative writers from the time of Disraeli onwards have recognized that a government must have policies, but have argued against deriving policies from a rigid ideological framework. In many respects, the Conservatives are a "catchall" party, ready to adopt a wide range of policies consistent with an anti-Socialist outlook. Insofar as the Conservative and Labour parties represent different class interests, these can be expected to result in the articulation of policies favouring the middle class and working class respectively.[7]

A second basic assumption is that it is possible to identify which "part" of a party determines its policies. In organizations as large as the Conservative or Labour parties, there are inevitably differences *within* as well as between the parties. These go well beyond the well-publicized differences generated by extreme statements by individual politicians such as Enoch Powell or, in a previous political existence, Michael Foot. Within the Conservative ranks, differing policy outlooks can be characterized by a variety of labels: *traditional, free market, socially conscious*, and so forth. Distinctive differences about particular policies in the Conservative ranks have not coalesced into organized and stable factions. In the Labour Party, by contrast, the difference between "left" and "right" or the *Tribune* or *Militant* left and Social Democrats is stable, and is backed up by factional organizations.[8]

Every party is dualist when in government, for there is inevitably a gulf between the party in office and the party outside the gates. Party members acting as Cabinet ministers are subject to a host of pressures and constraints that do not play upon backbench MPs, party headquarters or constituency activists. Nor can these pressures be ignored, because they immediately affect the political success of the Cabinet. The party outside the gates can only comprehend these pressures vicariously. Often, it is asked to accept that there are obstacles to realizing policies that those without experience of governing may not fully appreciate, and to trust the minister to do the best job he can for the party. If the distance between party rhetoric and government performance is substantial, differences within the governing party will widen, as disappointment leads the party outside government to become distrustful.

There are differences between the Conservative and Labour parties about which parts of the party ought to determine policy. The Conservative position is unambiguous; the leader of the party is the final authority in the enunciation of Conservative policy, whether in government or opposition. By contrast, Labour Party politicians disagree about the relative weight of the parliamentary and extraparliamentary parties. The victory at the 1979 Labour Conference of the left-wing proponents of extraparliamentary supremacy registered a shift in power between institutions that have disagreed about their respective roles for generations.[9]

Third, it is assumed that parties enunciate different policy intentions. If this is not done, then a general election is meaningless in policy terms, a choice between a more or less interchangeable Tweedledum and Tweedledee. Insofar as party competition is political and politics is about the articulation of conflicting demands, these conflicts are expected to be registered in the party system. The model of Westminster parliamentary government gives palpable form to this assumption. Government and opposition sit opposite each other as adversaries in the House of Commons, where they are expected to disagree about major issues of the day.

Parties can compete with each other by claiming to be more proficient in achieving goals generally valued by the electorate. For example, the Conservative and Labour parties do not compete by one party favouring full employment, and the other unemployment, or one favouring inflation and the other price stability. The parties compete by each claiming to be *better* qualified to achieve both full employment and stable prices. Instead of taking different positions, the parties take the same position, but differ in boasting of their competence in handling what Donald Stokes has termed "valence" issues, that is, conditions commonly valued by the majority of the electorate.[10] Parties can claim a greater likelihood of success in achieving common goals by offering different programme means. But the electorate may be less concerned with the particulars of programmes than it is with making a generalised judgment of the relative competence of the parties.

Politics is about reconciling as well as articulating differences. Insofar as there is a substantial majority in favour of a given policy, then differences can disappear as parties scurry to adopt the one position popular with the bulk of the voters. Parties designing policies similar to each other are like two automobile manufacturers offering potential customers a car that is identical in nearly all fundamental respects, differing only at those points where small advantages may be won without alienating anyone. Lord Hailsham has given unabashed testimony to the Conservatives' readiness to adopt the policies of opponents when this is tactically desirable:

> There is nothing immoral or even eccentric in catching the Whigs bathing and walking away with their clothes. There is no copyright in truth, and what is controversial politics at one moment may after experience and reflection easily become common ground.[11]

The greater the differences between parties about the basics of politics, the more "un-English" party competition seems. For example, in Italy the two major parties—the Communists and Catholics—have claimed to pursue mutually exclusive ideologies in the past[12] and beyond them are armed leftist and fascist groups that pursue their ends by terrorism and murder. Within the United Kingdom, Northern Ireland parties have differences so great that Parliament is not prepared to allow normal Westminster electoral or parliamentary procedures to govern the Province. The Loyalist parties and the Social Democratic and Labour parties differ about whether ultimate political authority should be vested in Westminster or Dublin, and paramilitary groups invoke the bullet instead of the ballot to arbitrate differences.[13]

A fourth basic assumption of representative government—the party winning an election will carry out its intentions in practice—posits that voters will not only be offered a choice but also that their choice makes a real difference in how society is governed. If this did not occur, parties could be accused of deluding the electorate in a competition for votes, or of idly indulging in ideological gratification, announcing intentions that will have no effect in practice.

In British politics, the doctrine of the mandate asserts that a party winning a general election has the *right* to carry out its policy intentions. The "professionalization" of politics in postwar Britain has invested greater effort in making policy statements, and enhances the presumptive weight of the policy intentions that parties put to the electorate in their manifestos.

The conventions of parliamentary democracy give the party that wins a majority of seats in the House of Commons complete control of government. In constitutional theory, this power admits no impediment. But in practice, a newly elected government does not necessarily have the power to achieve its intentions. If the electorate endorsed all the policies of a newly elected government, and it successfully put them all into practice, then most of the electorate should normally be satisfied with the government of the day. But this is not the case. The record of any party in office is normally a record of some intentions successfully realized and others abandoned. A party may gain popularity by abandoning policy intentions, just as it may unintentionally lose popularity by carrying out some of its manifesto pledges.

The party winning a general election can change the Cabinet, but there is much that it cannot change. The laws, spending commitments and personnel of government exert the inertia pressure of a great moving force. Those who step aboard the ship of state find that they are subject to powerful currents, and are not taking command of a passive or easily manoeuvred vessel. Upon entering office, a party becomes subject to demands from pressure groups that it might ignore in opposition. It must also confront international forces, economic as well as diplomatic, that greatly constrain government. In order to carry out its policy intentions, the governing party must not only have policies that are desirable in opposition but also "do-able" within the constraints of office.

The Historical Context

The best way to judge whether the Conservative and Labour parties pursue different policies is to study their records in office. The policies that parties enunciate in opposition are of limited importance, for when they are made they can have no immediate effect upon what government does. The policies that a party makes in office constitute a record of its political achievements, affecting the whole of the country. If there are substantial shifts in government policy when a party moves in and out of office, this is evidence of political differences about how the country should be governed. If the shifts are in accord with the intentions of the governing party, this is evidence that parties make the difference.

The best way to avoid the faults of generalizing from a single Parliament or a single Prime Minister is to study the alternation of parties in office over a substantial period of time. The study of a single government can always be challenged by the argument that "if only" the opposition had been in office, things would have been different. By definition, this hypothetical state never occurs. It is thus impossible to test empirically the familiar assertion that the other party would have done the same, if it could have been put in the same position. But it is possible to test what happens when, with the alternation of parties in office, a group of politicians who were formerly without responsibility takes direction of government.

The effect of parties rotating in office can best be examined in the period since 1957. The Labour and Conservative parties became the principal adversaries in British politics with the rise of Labour in the 1920s. But between the wars the Conservatives normally formed the government alone or in coalition. The period from 1940 until 1957 is atypical. In wartime, there was a coalition government of Conservatives, Labour and Liberals. Much of the foundation of the postwar welfare state was debated and agreed upon in coalition. The return of a Labour government in 1945 did not bring to power a party formerly in opposition, but a party that had shared power for five years previously. The Conservative governments under Winston Churchill and Anthony Eden from 1951 to 1956 were led by politicians concerned almost exclusively with foreign affairs. The abrupt departure from office of Anthony Eden in 1957 marked a watershed in British party politics.

Contemporary concerns of party politics began to emerge during the Prime Ministership of Harold Macmillan from 1957 to 1963. In 1957 the Conservative government established the first of what has become a continuing stream of councils, commissions and boards concerned with aspects of the economy: Lord Cohen's Council on Prices, Productivity and Income. The Radcliffe Committee on the Working of the Monetary System was also appointed in 1957, in recognition of the fact that something was "not quite right" with sterling. In international affairs, the Macmillan government presided over a post-Suez war review of defence followed by the scaling down of the country's military role, and sailed with the winds of change that meant the end of Britain's Imperial role. Macmillan took the first step towards Britain's entering the European Community.

The chapters that follow analyze evidence from seven Parliaments, five Prime Ministers and four different periods of party government, two Conservative and two Labour, from 1957 to Margaret Thatcher's accession to office in 1979. Where relevant data is available for the period since

1945, it is included; at other points, evidence may not cover the full time span because of practical difficulties in obtaining consistent data for very lengthy time periods. Because the evidence is particularly rich for the 1970s, it is therefore specially relevant as a prelude to understanding party government in Britain in the 1980s.

Conservative Government, 1957–64. The accession of Harold Macmillan to the Prime Ministership marked a major change in the direction of the Conservative Party. Macmillan had always been an outsider in the Conservative Party, and was much more concerned with economic and social issues than his foreign affairs minded predecessors, Winston Churchill and Anthony Eden. Moreover, Macmillan was an avowed Keynesian and was prepared to see his Treasury ministers resign as a group in 1958 when they objected to his wish to pursue a more expansionist economic policy. The Labour leader elected in 1955, Hugh Gaitskell, died unexpectedly in January 1962. Harold Wilson's accession to the Labour leadership changed the style but not the content of Labour's policy in opposition.

Labour Government, 1964–70. Labour's entry to office after thirteen years in opposition was an exceptionally good test of transition from opposition to office. Labour had long been preparing in anticipation of gaining office, and it expected to govern the nation differently from the allegedly "thirteen wasted years" of its Conservative predecessors. The Conservatives' prompt election of Edward Heath as party leader in August 1965 gave the opposition a new head. Following the Conservatives' decisive defeat in the March 1966 general election, there was ample time for the Labour government to write a record, and for the Conservatives to elaborate policy intentions in opposition, an opportunity that Heath seized.

Conservative Government, 1970–74. The Conservatives entered office in June 1970, with policy intentions (and, in some cases, draft legislation) prepared in opposition, reflecting Heath's belief in "Action not Words." The Prime Minister was determined not to continue what were seen as the mistakes of the 1964–70 Labour government. Because Labour remained under the leadership of Harold Wilson in opposition, the period also tests the extent to which a party led by ex-ministers tends to retain a frontbench view of public policy, rather than adopting a more carefree view of policy when out of office.

Labour Government, 1974–79. While the leadership of this Labour government was shared between Harold Wilson (1974–76) and James Callaghan (1976–79), its composition and policies were sufficiently consistent to justify treating it as one piece. During the latter part of the 1974–79 Parliament, Labour lost its absolute parliamentary majority, but this did not prevent it from pressing forward controversial bills (e.g., devolution), just as a large majority does not require a governing party to introduce controversial measures. The election in 1975 of a new Conservative leader, Margaret Thatcher, absolved the leadership from the need to defend the record of the 1970–74 Conservative government. Many Conservatives were anxious to distance themselves from the perceived shortcomings of the Heath administration. Moreover, Mrs. Thatcher's personal proclivity was to seek differences in principle between the opposition and government.

Persisting doubt and anxiety about "What's Wrong with Britain?" became evident in the period of Harold Macmillan's government.[14] Many of the problems that faced Britain in the 1950s remain familiar today because they have not been resolved by Conservative and Labour governments. Moreover, such problems as the management of the economy are perennial; the government of the day must always make decisions about how to encourage economic growth and minimize the risks of inflation and unemployment. Because of the continuity in the problems facing Britain since 1957, it is possible to compare how successive Conservative and Labour governments have responded to similar problems, and even to compare how the same party has reacted to similar difficulties at different times in office.

It can be argued that the period from 1957 to 1979 is atypical, differing from the interwar era of Conservative hegemony, and that a "new era" may have opened with the 1979 general election. Margaret Thatcher is ready to proclaim that the "old politics" is not only dead but discredited. The voices that dominated the 1979 Labour Party Conference are equally strong in rejecting the record of the past. In a literal sense, the past cannot predict the future. But past patterns of behaviour greatly limit what any government of the day can do. It cannot repeal wholesale the legislation of its predecessors, nor can it avoid the economic problems it inherits.

Like it or not, we must turn to the record of achievement rather than the rhetoric of intentions to see whether parties make a difference in the way Britain is governed. Insofar as parties do make a difference, voters should ponder carefully the choice they make before casting their ballot

17

for the government of Britain in 1984. Insofar as parties do not make a difference, politicians might consider whether this signifies that their policies are ill-advised or whether the problems of British society are not readily amenable to influence by any British government, whatever its political intentions.

CHAPTER 2

Adversary or Consensus Politics?

The conventional model of British government assumes that parties are adversaries. The Conservative and Labour parties are meant to oppose each other in parliamentary debates and at general elections, and to govern the country differently when each has its turn in office. The consensus model of party government rejects each of these assumptions. The Conservative and Labour parties, while opposing each other in Parliament and in general elections, are expected to agree about the fundamentals of governance and not to differ substantially in their policies. When each succeeds the other in office, major policies are assumed to remain much the same.

The *Adversary* model of party politics emphasizes the confrontation of parties in different positions, government and opposition, at the same point in time. In the most literal sense, the two parties cannot behave identically in such circumstances because the party in power is responsible for government while its opponent is confined to the weakness of opposition. Differences in policy are expected to follow from differences in position. Yet if the governing party pursues popular policies, opposition for its own sake would further weaken electoral support for a defeated party. Hence, there are tactical as well as principled grounds to expect a measure of consensus between parties in different positions, insofar as there are some policies that a majority of the electorate consistently favours.

The *Consensus* model of party politics emphasizes continuity between parties in the same position, government, at different points in time. It downgrades the significance of parliamentary competition because one of the competitors has no influence on government, whereas the other has the power of decision. When a party succeeds to office, it will adopt the same policies as its predecessor, even if it had been averse to them in opposition. The Consensus model assumes that the constraints of office are all-powerful. Whatever a party says in opposition, there is only one policy that a government can follow, whichever party is in office. The Adversary model, by contrast, implies that a party moving from opposition to office can and will adopt policies differing from its predecessor.

The purpose of this chapter is to consider systematically four logically different models of party competition. The models describe in idealized form how parties act under certain stipulated assumptions. They do not prescribe how parties should act, nor is it the purpose here to recommend one of these models as prescriptively best. Knowing where we are is important as a precondition for any effective prescription of what party politics ought to be like. The point of this study is to see which, if any, of these models best fits contemporary Britain. The first two concentrate attention on the behaviour of parties at the same point in time. The third and fourth models turn attention to the actions of parties at different points in time, as each succeeds to the powers and responsibility of government.

Government and Opposition

1. The Adversary Model of Party Policy

In a two-party system, with one party in office and the other in opposition, the Adversary model of party policy posits that at a given point in time,

Opposition intention is not equal to Government practice

The Adversary model expresses the contrast between the position of government and opposition. It assumes that the party out of office will wish to emphasize or even create disagreements about policy with the party in government. The disagreements may be tactical, seized upon momentarily for the sake of "making" differences. Or they may be strategic, arising from parties' differing principles or ideologies, or fundamentally different interests of their respective electoral constituencies. If a party out of office only endorsed what was said and done by the party in government, it would be redundant, offering voters little reason to turn the governing party out.

The traditional justification for parliamentary opposition assumes that good government requires open and searching debate about alternative policies in order to reach the best conclusion. The Adversary method of decision making is central in the common law system of justice, and Parliament opposed the government for centuries before the creation of the modern party system. In the nineteenth century, John Stuart Mill gave the classic justification for debate between adversaries as the best means of testing statements of fact and opinion. Ministers today accept the right of the opposition to challenge their actions, even when they find it inconvenient for Parliament to question and debate their policies. No British political party rejects the liberal case for the free competition of conflicting political ideas.

A second justification for parties opposing each other's policies is electoral. In Bernard Crick's phrase, *"Parliament primarily serves to inform the electorate, neither to legislate nor to overthrow Governments."*[1] Parties competing for electoral favour should compete against each other in the House of Commons. The parties may differ about the means or ends of policies or both. Each side will claim that its leaders are superior in competence to the leaders of the other team. The governing party will argue that the measures it adopts are the best possible in the circumstances, and the opposition will criticize the party in office for not doing as well as it would itself. On the basis of this confrontation at Westminster, the electorate is expected to decide which party can best govern the country.

The Adversary model has a third justification: The two major parties are based upon conflicting interests (trade unions and the working class vs. business and the middle class) and/or conflicting ideologies (e.g., Tory vs. Socialist). Differences in interests cause parties to formulate policies to reward or "pay off" their loyal supporters. For example, the Conservatives are expected to advance policies favouring business profits, and Labour, measures favouring trade union interests. Insofar as parties are "principled," as the vast literature about party philosophies implies, then the two parties should find themselves on opposite sides of issues that raise questions of principle.

The opposition can differ from the governing party by following either of two contrasting strategies.[2] It can act solely as a critic or it can differentiate itself by acting as an alternative government. The first strategy is aptly summed up in the dictum: The opposition's job is to oppose; that is, it should criticize government policies without offering any clue about what it would put in its place. In the words of Harold Macmillan:

It is bad enough having to behave like a government when one is a government. The whole point of being in opposition is that one can have fun and lend colour to what one says and does.[3]

The second strategy posits that the opposition should use its time out of office to reflect upon past mistakes and prepare plans for future achievements in office. By acting as an alternative government, a party might make a positive impression on the electorate, and also be well prepared for the challenge of office. The first strategy may sometimes be described as "irresponsible" opposition, and the latter as "too responsible" opposition.

There is a pragmatic, even responsible case for acting as an "irresponsible" opposition. It starts from the fact that the opposition lacks the resources of office. Without the information and advice of Whitehall, the opposition will not be fully informed of the variety of constraints that influence government policy. Without the ability to act promptly upon a statement of intent, the opposition may find that circumstances have changed greatly when it is next in office, and earlier commitments can become embarrassingly inappropriate. Moreover, without the discipline and patronage of office, the party leadership may, when announcing its intentions, succumb to strong pressures within the party and ignore pressures that could not be ignored in office. Insofar as such arguments are deemed convincing, an opposition's negativism does not so much reflect an absence of thought as a calculated belief that discretion is the better part of valour.

The argument for acting as an alternative government starts from the fact that electoral defeat indicates that the losing party has deficiencies it should remedy. Abandoning old policies and adopting new policies is one course of action it can take. To avoid formulating any distinctive policies is to leave the opposition open to criticism that it has nothing positive to offer in place of what the government is doing. The more the opposition believes that the governing party is making fundamental mistakes, the more likely opposition politicians will wish to prepare policies to put right what they believe to be wrong. Insofar as intraparty debate involves leading personalities jockeying for position in opposition, at a minimum they must use policies as an excuse for their differences. For example, Aneurin Bevan had to make himself the tribune of the left to challenge Herbert Morrison and Hugh Gaitskell for leadership of the Labour Party, and Enoch Powell had to enunciate policy differences with Edward Heath to justify breaking with him politically.

2. The Consensus Model of Party Policy

In a two-party system, the Consensus model flatly contradicts the adversary model, positing

Opposition intention is equal to *Government practice*

It assumes that at any given point in time the opposition will not, cannot or should not differ from the governing party of the day. The classic statement of this model was given by A. J. Balfour, an unusually philosophical Conservative Prime Minister, in an introduction to Walter Bagehot's *The English Constitution*, written shortly after the 1926 general strike:

> Our alternating Cabinets, though belonging to different parties, have never differed about the foundations of society. And it is evident that our whole political machinery pre-supposes a people so fundamentally at one that they can safely afford to bicker.[4]

Balfour argued that agreement between the parties was derived from sharing a common set of values.

The Consensus model emphasizes the things that politicians have in common, rather than the things that divide them. The *prima facie* differences that exist as a condition of electoral competition are said to be "not really" important, by comparison with the consensus said to exist on "fundamentals." The Consensus model is concerned with the basic values of the political culture, which support the institutions of the regime and the community to be governed, and set limits to legislation.[5] From a sufficiently lofty position, it could be argued that as long as all parties competing for office accept the Constitution, then differences on specific policies are of secondary concern.

The dislike of "factional" or "sectional" political differences has a historical tradition long antedating the liberalism of John Stuart Mill. In the seventeenth and eighteenth centuries, parties were viewed as factions creating conflicts in what was assumed to be an organic society with a consensual set of values. The outlook remains alive today in the intermittent calls from retired politicians and others for a renunciation of party politics and the co-option of nonparty leaders (e.g., themselves) into government.

In the 1974 crisis of party government, leaders of the Conservative and Labour parties both made references to the desirability of "national unity." Immediately after his October 1974 election victory, Harold Wilson appealed in a ministerial broadcast to "the whole of the national family" to accept "a partnership in which all of us should be partners and all must play their part." Wilson argued: "As we leave the election campaign behind us, our national task now is to concentrate on solving together the problems before us."[6] Nevertheless, neither Wilson nor Heath was prepared to sacrifice his position or party for the sake of a "national" government.

There is always a significant portion of the electorate favouring coalition government. For example in a spring, 1978 Opinion Research Centre poll, 47 percent said they thought an all-party coalition government a good idea, compared to 33 percent endorsing a single-party government pursuing conventional partisan policies.[7]

Practicing politicians are prepared to recognize the electoral appeal of Consensus insofar as an emphasis upon Adversary principles is divisive, and threatens to exclude support from a portion of the electorate. Harold Wilson, when leader of the Labour Party, invariably eschewed mentioning the word "Socialism" in a nationally televised election campaign broadcast, just as he would happily invoke it when addressing a conference of party faithful. Lord Carrington, a former Conservative Party chairman, also shies away from Adversary principles:

> Obviously I accept all the things that Conservatives stand for: free enterprise, the rights of individuals and so on. But I would be distrustful of converting them into hard and fast policies.
> What the party is really crying out for is success.[8]

Consensus parties can compete by turning politics into a contest of personalities or teams of leaders. Even if ends are agreed upon, there can be differences about which party's leaders are best able to direct government toward these agreed goals. The most influential modern statement of this view in Britain is found in R. T. McKenzie's *British Political Parties:* "The essence of the democratic process is that it should provide a free competition for political leadership."[9] McKenzie derives this constitutional prescription from Joseph Schumpeter's magisterial study of *Capitalism, Socialism and Democracy.* In Schumpeter's view, competition for office is everything, and party policies are only incidental to competition. Schumpeter argues that just as a "department store cannot be defined in terms of its brands," so "a party cannot be defined in terms of its principles." While accepting that parties might compete tactically by offering different "brand" policies, Schumpeter emphasizes that democratic government requires that "the effective range of political decision should not be extended too far."[10]

Consensus politics does not require complete agreement among voters. What it does presuppose is that the majority of the electorate does endorse a single, usually middle-of-the-road position. Insofar as both parties compete for the support of the same group of floating voters, and these are located in the middle of a left-right continuum, then the Conservative and Labour parties, although starting from different directions, would tend to adopt the same policies to appeal to the same group of median voters.[11] Insofar as a party does not do so and is penalized by losing an election, it will immediately face pressure to adopt popular policies endorsed by the government, if it wishes to win the next election.

Consensus politics does not require complete agreement within or between parties. The Conservative and Labour parties each embrace individuals and groups covering a wide spectrum of views, ranging from the far right to the centre in the case of the Conservatives, and from the far left to the centre in the Labour Party.[12] There is thus some overlap in a simple left-right distribution of partisans, even if the midpoint within each party is at a distance from the other. The Consensus model postulates that the logic of electoral competition will force each party to allow its "centrist" wing to shape policies, as a necessary condition of winning a parliamentary majority.

Carried to its logical extreme, the Consensus model implies a denial of politics, that is, conflict about policies in government. Harold Laski delivered a classic Marxist indictment of consensus politics in the 1930s. He started by accepting the analysis of Bagehot and Balfour, that "since 1689, we have had, for all effective purposes, a single party in control of the state." While admitting that the single party was divided into two wings, Laski argued that the Conservatives, Whigs, and later the Liberals, were fundamentally at one in their view of the economic and social order. The rise of the Labour Party threatened this consensus, Laski declared, for he saw it challenging the established social and economic order and shattering comforting but untenable assumptions of consensus theorists. Laski suggested that the widening "intellectual abyss between parties" could even lead to a "war of creeds" in which "armed philosophies . . . do battle with one another."[13]

Events since 1945 have shown both Marxists and non-Marxists that Labour and Conservative governments could alternate in office without creating party competition *à outrance*.[14] The failure of a "war of creeds" to occur in a literal or figurative sense does not mean that party politics is without disagreement about policies. Insofar as consensus is derived from tactical electoral necessities rather than agreement upon fundamentals, there is always scope for differences in fundamental values to lead politicians to disagree about what the electorate thinks and wants. These disagreements can arise within as well as between parties. For example, the 1979 Labour Party chairman, Frank Allaun, told the Party Conference that Labour's failure to win the May election was because the party had not been "Socialist" enough, while many parliamentary Labour leaders were analyzing its defeat as the result of the party appearing "too" Socialist.

The Test of Office

Party government in Britain is, first, about the alternation of Conservative and Labour parties in government. In order to test whether parties in practice agree or are adversaries, their activities must be studied for a period in which each writes a record in government.

3. The Manifesto Model of Party Policy

When two parties alternate in office, then for a given party,

$$\textit{Opposition intention (time 1)}$$
$$\text{is equal to}$$
$$\textit{Government practice (time 2)}$$

The Manifesto model differs from the two previous models in that it is concerned with the continuity of a party's policy from opposition to office. In opposition a party will set out policy intentions, and then put these intentions into practice upon entering office.[15] This is invariably assumed to happen in discussions of the Adversary model. But it does not follow that a party will necessarily act upon criticisms made in opposition once it is in office. Nor is it to be taken for granted that a party in office will find it easy to realize intentions pronounced in the luxury of opposition.

The Manifesto model has both normative and empirical justifications. Normatively, it starts from the assumption that elections should offer voters a choice between alternative ways of governing the country. For an election to be meaningful in policy terms, the parties must not only pledge different policies but also practice what they preach. If this does not happen, then a party gains office on a false prospectus; and so well entrenched are the Conservative and Labour parties by the British electoral system that there would be little hope of penalizing parties that practiced fraud.

The Manifesto model justifies the government of the day enacting policies against the determined opposition of its adversary in Parliament. A party that wins an election is said to have a mandate to enact the policy intentions stated in its manifesto. Just as the governing party is expected to be bound to its manifesto intentions, so the electorate—including those who voted for other parties—are bound to accept the implementation of the winner's pledges.

Empirically, the Manifesto model starts from the assumption that individuals and organizations do have political predispositions that influence the policies they prefer. They are not open (or empty) minded decision makers reacting empirically to events. As Michael Oakeshott notes, "purely empirical politics," sometimes assumed to negate the influence of party, "are not something difficult to achieve or properly to be avoided, they are merely impossible, the product of a misunderstanding."[16] A newly elected Labour or Conservative Cabinet could no more abandon the attitudes and predispositions of a political lifetime than it could abandon identification with the party that had placed its members there.

The predispositions of party politicians are strongest in shaping manifesto intentions. Ministers are likely to start from the assumption that manifesto intentions are practicable as well as desirable. The stronger they are as politicians vis-à-vis their civil servants, the more argument they will require before abandoning these intentions. Even if manifesto intentions prove difficult to realize in office, they cannot be abandoned easily by ministers who have formerly proclaimed them. As and when manifesto intentions are abandoned in the face of events, the very fact that a government is departing from its intentions will create difficulties within the party. It makes the leadership vulnerable to attack by the party faithful, as well as an object of derision by opponents for belatedly abandoning the "errors" of its past.

The normative case for the Manifesto is challenged by empirical evidence from the electorate. Conventional theories of popular government assume that the government of the day will win the votes of a majority of the voters and that a majority will also endorse the major policies it offers. But this is not necessarily the case. The winning party at a British general election gains less than half the popular vote, and it is unlikely to have a majority of the electorate endorse (or necessarily be aware of) major policy positions.

In effect, an election is not a referendum on dozens of manifesto pledges but a crude choice between two bundles of party policies. A party may short-circuit rather than amplify popular preferences by including in its election manifesto policies disliked by a majority of the electorate. A manifesto is not drawn up as a reflection of public opinion; it is the product of complex negotiations among interested politicians. It thus reflects what the party leadership can collectively agree to, or what one faction can force the other to accept. It is not necessarily an assessment of what the voters want.

The Manifesto model is an introverted model, for it emphasizes the internal decisions of a governing party when in opposition. It discounts the radical changes of outlook that result when a party moves from opposition to office. Even the most carefully prepared policies of opposition cannot fully comprehend all the influences that affect a party in government. In effect, the Manifesto model emphasizes the continuity of the party *qua* organization, and ignores the discontinuity introduced by the party changing from opposition to government.

4. The Technocratic Model of Party Policy
    When two parties alternate in office, this model posits:

Conservative government practice (time 1)
is equal to
Labour government practice (time 2)

The Technocracy model concerns different parties in the same position at different points in time. The Technocracy model does not necessarily reject the Adversary model of relations between government and opposition. Instead, it denies its primacy. It is not concerned with whether parties differ in debate when one is governing, and the other confined to announcing intentions in opposition. Instead, it concentrates upon whether Conservative and Labour governments differ in what they do in office.

The Technocracy model can be justified on negative grounds by the constraints of office. These may be assumed to be invariant and so strong that a new government can do nothing different from the last government. Alternatively, it may be assumed that even though situations are variable, at any one moment circumstances determine what government must do, and there is no pattern that parties can impose upon events, or

that social scientists can discern. The relationship between party intentions and actions is more or less random. (See chap. 7)

The worldly wise Walter Bagehot a century ago captured the scep-
tic's belief that technical constraints determine policies, not party intentions. He wrote then:

> And the end always is that a middle course is devised, which *looks* as
> much as possible like what was suggested in opposition, but which *is* as
> much as possible what patent facts—facts which seem to live in the office,
> so teasing and unceasing are they—prove ought to be done.[17]

The Technocratic view was equally well summed up by Mr. Reginald
Maudling, a Conservative economic minister for eleven years from 1953
until 1964. Shortly after going into opposition, he said of the successor
government's economic policies: "It is true the Labour government have
inherited our problems. They seem also to have inherited our solutions."[18]

A positive expression of technocratic government is found in the literature of decision theory, which outlines techniques for optimal decision
making and policy optimization. Insofar as there are means to ascertain
precisely what the best possible choice or mix of policies is in a given situation, then all "rational" politicians should adopt the same policy.

Technology makes statements of the sort, if you want to do X, then
adopt policy Y, without prescribing a choice between alternative ends.
There was a period in postwar economic policy making when the Keynesian model of the economy was thought to tell politicians what they
needed to know and do in order to achieve a given tradeoff between unemployment and inflation. The "only" thing the government of the day
had to decide was what would be the politically most acceptable combi-
nation of inflation and unemployment rates.

For a period in the 1950s and 1960s, there were suggestions that a
Technocratic consensus was forming about major ends and means of
public policy. *The Economist* coined the word "Butskellism" (a compound of the names of R. A. Butler and Hugh Gaitskell, Conservative
and Labour Chancellors), to identify a presumed agreement across party
lines among frontbench leaders in both parties.[19] In the 1964 general
election, both major parties emphasized the primary importance of
achieving economic growth; they differed only about whether a "scientific" Socialist party led by Harold Wilson or a non-Socialist Conservative government would be better able to produce the desired results.

But British politics in the 1980s challenges any simple assertion of
Technocratic consensus about economic ends. The left-wing of the

Labour Party, sometimes invoking Marxist slogans, is a far cry from the free market wing of the Conservative Party. Moreover, the idea of a neutral and effective technology has been deflated by economic events. Since 1973, the coincidence of economic stagnation and a high level of price inflation has indicated that there is something seriously wrong with the Keynesian paradigm for steering the economy. Pulling the levers as instructed no longer produces the predicted or desired result.

Scientific decision making is a chimera because it makes assumptions about consensus that, by definition, cannot be met whenever a political, as distinct from a technical, problem arises. It may be possible to use policy optimization techniques to allot car-parking spaces in a new government building or inventory stores at a military base. But these techniques cannot dictate what should be done about problems subject to the normal play of conflicting values and interests.[20]

Just as the Manifesto model emphasizes continuity within a party as it changes place in politics, so the Technocracy model emphasizes continuity within government, notwithstanding a change of parties. Both models have a common weakness, namely, a tendency to downgrade the importance of the environment of public policy. This can be a dynamic force for unexpected change, upsetting the plans of partisans who believe manifestos can be timeless blueprints for action, and technocrats who find events undermining the assumptions of theories from which their prescriptions are deduced.

The Contingency of Influence

The relationship between parties and public policy is contingent, not certain. Each of the models of party government presented here offers a number of hypotheses about how parties *might* behave; they present a recognizable and not implausible picture of what can happen in Britain today. None of the models need be wholly true or false. We should therefore ask: Under what circumstances are different models most likely to be true?

Differences between parties provide one possible explanation for the variable applicability of these models. Conventionally, the Labour Party sees itself as a party conforming to the Adversary and Manifesto models of governing. The Labour Party was founded to challenge fundamental characteristics of the society of pre-1914 England, and its Constitution and ideology proclaim that its leaders should give effect to the policy intentions approved by Party Conferences and stated in its election manifesto. By contrast, the Conservative Party has enunciated the ideology of a Consensus party. It may do so as a matter of national interest; for reasons of class interest, that is, a working-class party should not disagree with it; or by "borrowing" policies from its opponents that are popular with the electorate. Some contemporary Conservatives see their party as Technocratic, adopting the most efficient and best means of managing the economy because of a pragmatic openness to experiment, *or* because the market economy, as ideology and practical prescription, is believed to be technocratically superior to the prescriptions of Socialism.

The extent to which different models are applicable can vary with the "part" of the party to which it is applied. The Adversary and Manifesto models appeal most to the extraparliamentary party: constituency activists who gain "psychic" gratification from party controversy in Parliament as a reward for their voluntary efforts, and loyal voters who expect material benefits from the implementation of manifesto pledges in their interest. Since a majority of the electorate does not vote for the party in power, voters might favour the Consensus model. Electors might wish the governing party to move slowly, to be sure of general approval rather than quickly carrying out manifesto pledges that could go against the wishes of a majority of voters. Technocracy appeals most to frontbench politicians who seek a philosopher's stone that will assure them continuing success in office.

The position a party occupies in a given Parliament also affects the model describing its behaviour. The governing party of the day can find both the Consensus and the Technocracy models useful. The latter implies that there is only one way in which the country can be governed (the policies that it determines as the government), and the former suggests that the opposition should not voice major disagreement with the government's actions. The Adversary and Manifesto models are well suited to the position of the opposition party. The Adversary model justifies the opposition criticizing the governing party on all occasions, and the Manifesto model promises the party faithful that policies that cannot be put into effect in the present Parliament will become binding in the next.[21]

The cycle of activities in each Parliament also influences the applicability of these models of party government. When a newly elected government enters office, it may be anxious to carry out the pledges in its manifesto, believing that this will be as easy to do in Whitehall as it was in a party conclave. After a year, the governing party may instead be looking for technocratically effective ways to govern the country, whether or not the policies prescribed follow manifesto pledges. A party ejected from office may initially be surprised by defeat, and its frontbench spokesmen may voice Consensus views because they are still thinking like government ministers. Once the reality of defeat has become apparent, the same opposition spokesmen (or their successors) may turn to Adversary policies, as the midterm slump in popularity of the governing party lends credibility to the opposition's claim "There must be a better way." As an election approaches, the opposition may intensify its differences or, if it senses a shift in political climate, appeal to the electorate by claiming Technocratic superiority or a greater ability to achieve a national Consensus.

A sceptical historian might argue that while these models of party behaviour are logically clear, their relevance is unpredictable, for the actions of parties at a given time are dictated by the situation. A change of individual leaders or an unexpected event—the three-day week or a threat of war—may completely change how a party acts in office or in opposition. If this be true, then there should be no discernible pattern in the events of two decades analyzed here.

Even though each of the above models is plausible and under certain circumstances may be true, all of them cannot be equally true. The Adversary and Manifesto models could both be consistently true, for both emphasize differences between parties. Similarly, the Consensus and Technocracy models emphasize what parties have in common. But two models that assume that parties are different and two that stress similarities cannot all fit the same set of facts.

The chapters that follow test these models against different features of the practice of party government. Chapter 3 tests whether parties follow an Adversary or Consensus course when competing in a general election. The extent to which the Manifesto is acted upon is the issue in chapter 4. Chapter 5 tests whether the parties act in an Adversary or Consensus manner when they face each other in Parliament. The suitability of the seemingly neutral topic of government reorganization for Technocratic determination is tested in chapter 6. Chapter 7 examines, rigorously and in detail, whether anything approximating Technocracy is used by parties to manage the economy.

CHAPTER 3

The Choice at Elections

Since parties are meant to represent the electorate, the views of voters should be fundamental in determining whether parties follow an Adversary or a Consensus path. Insofar as those who vote for different parties hold different opinions about issues, then the parties should be Adversaries, offering the electorate a choice of policies. Insofar as those voting for different parties hold the same views on issues, then the parties should express a Consensus, advocating common policies reflecting the electorate's broad agreement.

Every general election demonstrates that voters differ in at least one respect: which party they wish to represent them. At no general election in Britain since 1935 has one party secured as much as half the popular vote. If the winning party's vote is calculated as a share of the total registered electorate, then the winning party receives the support of little more than one-third of the electorate. The mechanics of the electoral system reduce the effective adversaries. In the characteristic words of a *Times* 1959 election leader: "The country has to be governed and there is no escaping the fact that one of the two sides must do it."

Differences expressed in the polling booths do not necessarily reflect different views of public policy. After all, even though Presbyterians, Methodists, Anglicans and Catholics go to different churches, they read the same Bible and, presumably, pray to the same God. Similarly, British voters may support different parties, but they share much in common about how the country ought to be governed. Hence, the first part of this chapter examines the extent to which people voting for different parties hold Consensus or Adversary views on major policy issues.

The party that wins a general election enjoys all the powers of government, including the right of deciding what the voters get. Instead of consulting public opinion polls to see what the voters think, it can follow its own ideas about what is best for the country. The second section of

this chapter therefore examines whether during an election campaign parties show an Adversary or Consensus approach to government.

What the Voters Think

The British electorate is said to be socially homogeneous, but this statement does not imply Consensus politics. The electorate is described as homogeneous because class differences are the only (*sic*) thing said to differentiate Conservative and Labour voters. According to many political theories, class differences should produce intense policy differences between Labour, regarded as the party of the working class, and the Conservatives, regarded as the party of the middle class. As British elections involve class-based parties competing for popular votes, it should follow that the Adversary model best describes how the electorate lines up.

In fact, the British electorate is *not* divided on class lines in the simple way that the Adversary model implies.[1] Consistently, at election after election, surveys show that both the middle and the working classes divide votes (table 3.1). In 1979, *less than half* (46 percent) of manual workers or their families voted Labour, only 8 percent more than the proportion voting Conservative. The middle class is more cohesive than

TABLE 3.1   *Class Differences in Party Loyalties, 1979*

	Conservative %	Labour %	Liberal and Nationalist* %	As % Total
Middle Class				
A Professional	70	13	17	2
B Businessmen	61	19	20	12
C1 Lower middle	53	28	19	23
All middle class	57	25	19	36
Working Class				
C2 Skilled manual	41	42	17	33
D Semiskilled	33	50	17	22
E Very poor	39	48	13	9
All working class	38	46	16	64

*The Nationalists (3.2 percent) are included with the Liberals (14.0 percent) in order to show the proportions of each class voting for "third force" parties.

SOURCE: Author's reanalysis of unpublished 1979 Gallup poll election surveys. The N of 8,106 excludes all who did not report voting or give a party inclination.

the working class, with a majority (57 percent) voting Conservative, but it too shows internal divisions; three in seven middle-class voters support Labour, the Liberals or Nationalists. The most cohesive group is the overwhelmingly Conservative upper middle class, but it constitutes only 2 percent of the total electorate. As one descends the social ladder within the middle class, the Conservative predominance reduces; in the largest stratum, the lower middle class, little more than half favour the Conservatives. Within the working class, there are also divisions, for skilled manual workers—one-third of the electorate—divided almost evenly between the two major parties in the 1979 election, whereas Labour had a 3–2 advantage over the Conservatives among semiskilled workers.

The conventional picture of a Labour voter as a manual worker who is a trade unionist, council house tenant, poorly educated and thinks of himself as working class provides a very limited understanding of the behaviour of the total electorate. Ideal-type manual workers do vote Labour by a margin of almost three to one, but they constitute less than one-tenth of the electorate. Half of Labour's voters lack at least *two* of these ideal-type characteristics.[2] A larger proportion of the middle class conforms to the stereotype of a middle-class person: a homeowner, having more than the minimum of education, not belonging to a trade union, engaged in nonmanual work and thinking of himself as middle class. Among this eighth of the electorate, three-quarters vote Conservative. The extent of class-determined party loyalties is further reduced by the fact that three-quarters of the electorate do not match fully the stereotypes of class, and are less likely to conform to class stereotypes in voting.

A summary test of the influence of all class-related influences (e.g., trade union membership, council house residence, occupation) can be obtained by seeing what proportion of the total vote these influences predict altogether when analyzed by a sophisticated multivariate statistical technique known as Tree Analysis (AID). Insofar as party loyalties are class determined, as the Adversary model suggests, then class-related social differences should explain upwards of half the variation in party choice between Conservative and Labour voters. But insofar as party choice cuts across class lines, as the Consensus model predicts, then class-related social difference should account for much less than half the variation in the vote.

In seven elections since 1959, Gallup poll surveys show that the great majority of the vote cannot be explained in simple class terms.[3] Altogether, the host of class-related influences leave *un*explained four-fifths to seven-eighths of the difference between Conservative and Labour

35

voters.[4] When allowance is made for the fact that this excludes those voting for the Liberals or Nationalists and abstainers, the proportion of the vote of the total electorate that can be statistically explained in class terms drops to less than one-eighth of the total.[5]

There is a tendency for the influence of class-related differences to be declining, when the same statistical methods are applied to the same series of Gallup data. In 1959, 21.1 percent of the combined Conservative and Labour vote could be explained by class-related social differences; in 1979, the proportion was 12.3 percent. The decline in turnout and voting for the two major parties means that whereas class differences could statistically explain the actions of 15.6 percent of the 1959 electorate, in 1979 the same influences could only account for 7.7 percent of the actions of the electorate. By international standards, the British electorate shows a relatively low degree of division into Adversary groups opposing each other on class lines.[6]

Even though the Conservative and Labour parties are often described as class adversaries, the electorate does not line up like a pair of boxers facing each other. Instead, when analyzed in terms of joint class and party alignments, the bulk of the electorate must be divided into four unequal groups, like two unevenly matched pairs in a golfing foursome — plus groups of Liberal and Nationalist supporters wishing to challenge the foursome.

The two largest sociopolitical groups in the British electorate are both working class, the 27 percent that votes Labour and the 23 percent that votes Conservative. The third largest group consists of middle-class Conservatives (19 percent), which is much larger than the fourth, middle-class Labour voters (8 percent). Liberals and Nationalists add to the fragmentation by drawing a "third force" vote in both middle and working classes, and the extent of class voting is further diluted by those electors who deny a willingness to vote or any party inclination when interviewed.[7] According to Gallup poll data, less than half (46 percent) of the British electorate in 1979 conformed to the familiar Adversary stereotypes of middle-class Conservative or working-class Labour voters.

The social structure of the electorate would doom the Conservatives to unending defeat if the party became identified as the protagonist of the middle class and the adversary of the working class. In practice, the Conservatives have always been able to sustain a cross-class (or, party leaders would say, a "national") appeal.[8] At every general election, the Conservatives draw about half their vote from working-class electors; in 1979, the Gallup poll reported that 54 percent of Conservative voters were working class (See table 3.2). For the Conservatives to oppose measures that were against the interests of the *whole* of the working class (and not just the trade union half of it) would threaten electoral suicide.

TABLE 3.2   *How the Electorate Divides by Class and Party, 1979*

	Conservative %	Labour %	Liberal and Nationalist %	Non-voters %
Middle Class				
A Professional	1.0	0.2	0.2	0.1
B Businessmen	6.7	2.0	2.2	0.7
C1 Lower middle	11.4	5.9	4.0	1.6
All middle class	19.1	8.1	6.4	2.4
Working Class				
C2 Skilled manual	12.7	12.9	5.1	2.4
D Semiskilled	6.9	10.3	3.5	1.6
E Very poor	3.1	3.7	1.1	0.8
All working class	22.7	26.9	9.7	4.8

SOURCE: Author's reanalysis of unpublished 1979 Gallup poll election surveys.

Theoretically, the Labour Party could win elections by rejecting middle-class support completely and mobilizing three-quarters of the working class to vote on Adversary lines. In practice, Labour has not appealed solely to one class since 1918, when it adopted a Constitution making it a party appealing to all "workers by hand or by brain" (Clause IV.4), that is, virtually the whole of the electorate except for the relatively few with large sums of capital. Moreover, the Labour Party has never succeeded in creating a working-class consensus in support of its policies and candidates. Because Labour draws the vote of only half the working class, it is not *the* party of manual workers but *a* party drawing most of its vote from the working class. The same is also true of such minorities as the Communists and the National Front. In the 1979 election, *the Conservatives and Liberals too were working-class parties*, for the Liberals drew 58 percent of their vote and the Conservatives 54 percent from manual workers (table 3.2).

Overall, the social composition of the Conservative and Labour vote tends to reduce the potential for Adversary class politics. The Conservatives cannot champion the middle class against the working class without risking that portion of their vote that makes the difference between Labour in government and Labour in opposition.

Given that there remain some class differences in the profile of support for the Conservative and Labour parties, in making policy each party might favour the "interests" of the class more closely identified with it. For example, many debates about housing policy are not about whether new houses should be built but about what kinds of houses should be built and how they should be financed. Conservatives favour building for owner-occupiers, whose mortgages are subsidized by tax relief on interest payments; Labour favours building council houses subsidized through local authority rates. The proportion of new housing built for owner-occupiers or council tenants has tended to swing back and forth, according to whether there is a Conservative or Labour government.

But deriving policies from class interests is not so simple as it sounds. There are many policies that do not immediately touch class interests. Moreover, even when such interests can be identified or imputed, the governing party has the choice of adopting a policy that suits a majority of its supporters or of trying to increase its appeal where it has previously been weak (e.g., Conservatives appealing to manual workers, and Labour to the middle class).

The consensual push toward overlapping if not identical policies is illustrated by the way the two parties actually deal with housing in government. The Labour Party does not make itself the adversary of owner-occupiers, by repealing laws granting tax relief on interest paid for mortgages. To do so would be consistent with many Socialist beliefs, but it would also be against Labour's immediate electoral interests, since owner-occupiers far outnumber council house tenants and constitute a majority of the electorate. Equally, Conservatives do not stop the building of council houses or end all housing subsidies to renters, for nearly one-quarter of Conservative voters are council house tenants.[9]

If electors vote according to how they think rather than who they are, then they will vote according to their policy preferences and not their social characteristics. The contrasting editorial slants of the *Daily Telegraph* and the *Guardian* are evidence of differences in political opinions within the middle class, as the *Daily Mirror* and the *Express* reflect different views within the working class. It is both parsimonious and plausible to expect that those who vote Labour agree with each other and differ from Conservatives in their political views. This is what the Adversary model implies. Insofar as people who vote for different parties hold the same opinions about the most important issues of the day, their policy preferences conform to the Consensus model.

The simplest test of the models is to see whether a majority of Conservative voters line up on one side of an issue and a majority of Labour supporters line up on the other side. If so, then the two groups of partisans are adversaries. But if a majority of both Conservative and Labour voters have the same view of an issue, this supports the Consensus model. Because some voters will always respond "don't know" to a question, sometimes there may be no clearcut majority opinion within one or both parties, thus giving more leeway to party leaders.

During the 1979 general election campaign, national opinion polls asked a nationwide sample of voters their views about a wide range of political issues. The survey showed attitudes varying from national consensus to major divisions, depending on the issue. On some matters, such as heavier sentences for violent criminals, the electorate was almost unanimous. On other issues, such as the payment of social security benefits to the families of strikers, it was almost evenly divided (see table 3.3).

An absolute majority of the electorate endorsed the Conservative Party position on eight out of ten issues, and a plurality endorsed a ninth policy. Only one policy associated with Labour—withdrawal from the Common Market—was favoured by a bare majority of 50 percent, and that was not even official Labour policy in the 1979 election campaign (see tables 3.3 and 3.4). Given that the Conservatives won the 1979 election, agreement between the winning party and the electorate is easily understandable. In principle, it could reflect Adversary or Consensus politics.

In 1979, the electorate tended to hold consensual positions. A majority or plurality of Labour voters agreed with Conservative policies on seven of the ten issues analyzed here (tables 3.3 and 3.4). Agreement was registered not only on moral issues that parties usually avoid, such as the punishment of criminals, but also on policies that would be expected to show partisan differences in interest and ideology, such as the sale of council houses and nationalizing banks. Only one issue divided a majority of Labour voters from a majority of Conservative voters: whether to stop social security payments to strikers' families. Overall, Conservative supporters show themselves more "opinionated" than Labour supporters; on average only 11 percent of Conservatives were without an opinion, compared with 20 percent of Labour voters.

TABLE 3.3   *The Policy Preferences of Partisans during the 1979 Election*

| | Conservatives | | Labour | |
| Policy | Agree | Disagree | Agree | Disagree |
	%	%	%	%
Heavier sentences for violence and vandalism (CONSENSUS)	95	2	91	5
Compulsory secret ballots in unions before strike (CONSENSUS)	85	7	79	10
Stop sales of council houses to occupants (CONSENSUS)	17	73	20	65
Nationalize the banks (CONSENSUS)	7	80	14	52
Bring back grammar schools (CONSENSUAL)	80	8	41	32
Abolish closed shops (CONSENSUAL)	76	10	45	30
Abolish the House of Lords (CONSENSUAL)	13	65	29	29
Encourage more private medicine alongside the Health Service (DISAGREE)	66	19	40	45
Take Britain out of Common Market (DISAGREE)	42	46	58	30
Stop social security payments to strikers' families (ADVERSARY)	60	29	31	55

NOTE: Agree answers combine those strongly and slightly in favour; disagree answers, those slightly or strongly opposed; total answers do not add to 100 percent because of the exclusion of don't knows.

CONSENSUS issues show at least half in each party holding the same view, and CONSENSUAL issues that the largest single group in each party (but not half) take the same view.

ADVERSARY issues show at least half in each party holding opposite views; and DISAGREE issues that the largest single group in each party (but not half) take opposite views.

SOURCE: NOP, *Political Social Economic Review* (London: NOP, No. 19, 1979), pp. 21–22, and unpublished data supplied by NOP.

The extent of agreement between Conservative and Labour voters can be measured by an Index of Disagreement. If Conservative and Labour voters disagreed totally with each other, then the interparty Index of Disagreement would be 100. If they were totally in agreement, the Index of Disagreement would be zero. As a rule of thumb, partisans could be considered adversaries if the index was 50 or more, and tending toward consensus as the index declined towards zero. In 1979, the Index of Disagreement between Conservative and Labour voters was only 18 percent, showing a high overall level of consensus between voters in the two parties (see table 3.4). On no issue did the index reach 40 percent, and on four issues it was 7 percent or less.

The conclusions drawn from this 1979 election survey are consistent with findings from similar analyses of public opinion conducted in earli-

TABLE 3.4   *Interparty Disagreement and Intraparty Cohesion on Issues, 1979*

Policy	Interparty Index of Disagreement (higher = more disagreement)	Intraparty Cohesion % Cons. (higher =	% Labour more cohesion)
Stop sales of council houses	3	56	(45)
Heavier sentences for violence and vandalism	4	93	(86)
Compulsory secret ballots before strike	6	78	(69)
Nationalize the banks	7	73	(38)
Abolish the House of Lords	16	52	0
Take Britain out of Common Market	16	4	28
Encourage more private medicine	26	47	5
Stop social security payments to strikers' families	29	31	24
Abolish closed shops	31	66	15
Bring back grammar schools	39	72	9
Average, 10 policies	18	57	14*

NOTE: The interparty difference is the difference between the favourable answers given by Conservative and Labour supporters.

   Intraparty cohesion is the difference between those favouring and those opposing a policy within a party.

*Calculation excludes four bracketed ( ) scores for policies where a majority of Labour voters agreed with Conservative voters.

SOURCE: As in table 3.3.

er years.[10] In all these surveys the Conservatives appear as doubly a Consensus party. First, Conservative Party policies have tended to be in agreement with a majority of the electorate more often than the policies of the Labour Party. Second, Conservative Party supporters are more likely to agree with each other than are Labour supporters. This is shown by the Index of Intraparty Cohesion. The cohesion of each party can be measured by subtracting the proportion within a party opposed to a policy from the proportion favouring it. If partisans were aligned 100 percent in favour of a policy and zero against, the cohesion index would be 100; if they divided 50–50, the index would be zero; and if opinion within a party divided 75 to 25 percent, the index would be 50. An index number of 50 or more is evidence of a high degree of Consensus within a party on an issue. Overall, Conservative voters show Consensus on seven out of ten issues, with an average score of 57 percent on the Index of Intraparty Cohesion (table 3.4). Only one issue — the Common Market — divides Conservative voters into two nearly equal groups.

Insofar as policy issues create Adversaries, the greatest tensions today are found *within* the ranks of the Labour Party. Ironically, Labour voters are most likely to unite when they are in agreement with a majority of Conservative voters (e.g., about punishing criminals, secret ballots before strikes, selling council houses and opposing bank nationalization). On these four Consensus issues, the cohesion of Labour voters averages 60 percent. On the three issues about which Labour voters tend to disagree with Conservatives — withdrawal from the Common Market, encouraging private medicine, and stopping social security payments to strikers' families — Labour voters also fail to agree among themselves. Labour voters register a cohesion score of only 19 percent when they show a tendency to go along with Labour Party policy. Divisions on issues among Labour voters are not new; a comparison with opinion surveys of a decade earlier suggests that, if anything, the divisions may be growing greater.

All in all, the behaviour and policy preferences of voters reject the Adversary model and support the Consensus model of party government. Class differences determine only a limited proportion of votes. Both parties depend for electoral victory upon cross-class electoral support. Changes of votes within as well as between classes tend to determine election outcomes. Notwithstanding different voting habits, a majority of Conservative and Labour voters are likely to agree rather than disagree about a wide range of issues. Insofar as the parties follow cues from the electorate, they will follow the Consensus model.

What the Parties Think

The conventional view of elections follows the Adversary model of party government. For an electoral choice to be meaningful in policy terms, the parties should present differing prescriptions for government policies. But this expectation will be ill-founded if parties give priority to another convention of representative government, namely, that they should represent the voters. Insofar as voters tend to agree about major policy issues, then the parties should emphasize the same policy intentions, differing only about which party is more competent to achieve Consensus goals.

At every general election, the majority of voters see the parties as offering "a choice, not an echo." During each campaign, the Gallup poll asks a sample of the electorate: "Do you think that there are any really important differences between the parties, or are they all much of a muchness?" When the question was first asked in the early 1950s, both the Labour and Conservative parties sought to draw sharp distinctions between each other in terms of their Socialist or anti-Socialist stance. At that time, nearly three-quarters of the electorate thought that there was a difference between the parties (see table 3.5). After thirteen years of Conservative government and a period of revisionism in the Labour Party under Hugh Gaitskell, the proportion seeing the parties as different fell to 59 percent in the 1964 election campaign and has remained near that level at each election since.

The proportion of voters seeing the parties as "all much of a muchness" has increased steadily through the years, from 20 percent at the

TABLE 3.5 *Voters' Perceptions of Differences or Similarities between the Parties, 1951–79*

	1951	1955	1959	1964	1966	1970	Feb 1974	Oct 1974	1977	1979
					(in percent)					
Are important differences	71	74	66	59	55	54	57	54	34	54
Much of a muchness	20	20	29	32	37	41	38	41	60	41
Don't know	9	6	5	9	8	5	5	5	6	5
Balance (Is a difference less much of a muchness)	51	54	37	37	18	13	19	13	(-26)	13

SOURCES: 1951–66: Monica Charlot, *La Démocratie a l'Anglàise* (Paris: Armand Colin, 1972), p. 166; Gallup Poll, *Political Index* (monthly).

October 1951 general election, in which the *Mirror* headlined the electoral choice as *Whose finger do you want on the trigger?* to 41 percent in May 1979. Moreover, there is consistent evidence that election campaigns increase popular perceptions of differences between parties. For example, when the Gallup poll asked voters in May 1977 how they saw the parties, 60 percent reported them to be "much of a muchness" as against 34 percent perceiving a difference.[11] In other words, campaign differences between the parties are noticeable—but they now seem to be ephemeral.

During an election campaign, a party first of all presents itself as an organization; it is a team of candidates seeking office. On a minimalist definition of party competition, it need do nothing else than establish that the "blue" side is different from the "red" side. To interpret an election as a choice between ideologies is to misunderstand the nature of both parties and ideologies. A political party is not a thinking organization. Political philosophers may manufacture ideologies as a logically coherent set of ideas. But parties do not make ideologies in any positively identifiable sense, for the institutions that constitute a party are multiple and intellectually not coherent, nor are election organizers interested in philosophical matters.

A general election campaign is about a choice between organizations, not ideas. A party may even wish to avoid stressing distinctive principles or policies if it believes that these are unpopular with the electorate. For example, Conservatives are well advised not to speak in praise of inequality and rewarding the able few in an election whose outcome is determined by the votes of the masses. And Labour consistently avoids discussing redistributing incomes, for those with above the median income (by definition half the electorate) are more likely to vote.

A party will be tempted to sidestep any discussion of policies and emphasize personalities instead if its leader is more popular than his opponent, as Labour did in 1964, when Harold Wilson was perceived as more popular than Sir Alec Douglas-Home. The incentive to do so was even stronger in 1979 when Jim Callaghan led Margaret Thatcher in public opinion, but Conservative policies were more popular than Labour policies.

During an election campaign, the party and its leaders must say something. The party publishes a general election manifesto, and each parliamentary candidate normally produces an election address. When party leaders appear on television, they must give some indication of the political views or "image" that differentiates them from each other in appeals to the electorate. It is in "subphilosophical" materials that evidence must be sought about the Adversary or Consensus choice that the parties present to the electorate.

The mass of voters are not interested in the fine print of party pro-grammes any more than they are concerned with the nuances of philo-sophical debate. Down through the years, the Gallup poll consistently reports that voters are concerned with a few relatively broad issues of wide-ranging significance; peace, prosperity and economic security. In assessing the parties, voters do not so much scrutinize particular policies; instead they form a general judgment of what the parties appear to stand for.

In presenting their election manifesto, party leaders can characterize in a single simple phrase what they offer the electorate. The titles of party manifestos since 1945 are anodyne in the extreme. They consistently re-flect Consensus rather than Adversary themes (see table 3.6). There is nothing divisive about asking for *A Better Tomorrow* or *Let Us Face the Future*. To declare *This Is the Road* or *The Better Way* is to reveal nothing about the political direction in which a party leads. Nor is it easy to infer any ideological bias in the 1970 Labour declaration for a "strong" Britain, or the 1974 Conservatives talk of "firm" action. Most titles pre-sent propositions that it is politically impossible to oppose. For example,

TABLE 3.6   *The Consensual Titles of Party Manifestos, 1945–79*

	Conservatives	Labour
1945	Mr. Churchill's Declaration of Policy	Let Us Face the Future
1950	This Is the Road	Let Us Win Through Together
1951	Britain Strong and Free	Labour Party Election Manifesto
1955	United for Peace & Progress	Forward with Labour
1959	The Next Five Years	Britain Belongs to You
1964	Prosperity with a Purpose	Let's Go with Labour for the New Britain
1966	Action Not Words	Time for Decision
1970	A Better Tomorrow	Now Britain's Strong—Let's Make It Great to Live In
Feb. 1974	Firm Action for a Fair Britain	Let Us Work Together
Oct. 1974	Putting Britain First	Britain Will Win with Labour
1979	The Conservative Manifesto 1979	The Labour Way Is the Better Way

SOURCE: F. W. S. Craig, *British General Election Manifestos, 1900–1974* (London: Macmillan, 1975).

in 1966 the Conservatives could not argue that they were against making decisions (cf. Labour's *Time for Decision*) nor could Labour respond to the Conservative plea for *Action Not Words* by promising *Words Not Action*. Only the use of the party's name and colour gives an indication of which party's policies lie within the cover of the typical manifesto.

Opening an election manifesto immediately reveals highly specific statements about what government ought to do. The manifesto provides cues from party leaders to media commentators and constituency campaigners, and through them, the mass electorate, about the party's orientation to the chief problems facing the country (see chapter 4).

The distance between the Conservative and Labour parties' manifestos is narrowing through the years. An elaborate factor analysis by David Robertson of major themes in British election manifestos from 1924 through 1966 identified their most important persisting political dimension as the debate about economic policies and goals (e.g., the desirability of free market or Socialist economic policies).[12] Figure 3.1 shows how the manifesto views of the Labour and Conservative parties have changed through time on this economic dimension. The parties

Figure 3.1   The Narrowing Distance between Party Manifestos on Major Economic Issues, 1924–66

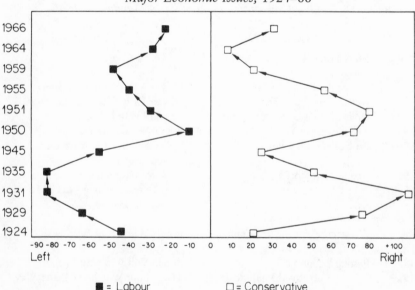

■ = Labour   □ = Conservative

Source: Adapted from David Robertson, *A Theory of Party Competition* (London: Wiley, 1976), p. 98.

were at the extremes in 1931, in the face of a major political and economic crisis. The two parties moved closer together up to 1945; the Conservatives after their election defeat immediately swung to the right. Upon returning to office in 1951, Conservative manifestos moved toward the middle on economic policy, whereas Labour statements swung left in opposition. The two both converged toward the centre in the mid-1960s. By 1964, the distance between the two parties on major manifesto economic issues was one-fifth that of 1931, according to Robertson's measure. The general message is clear: There has been a major long-term shift from Adversary towards Consensus outlooks in the principal campaign documents of the parties.[13]

More detailed confirmation of the move towards Consensus from 1945 to 1970 is provided by a systematic content analysis of party manifestos undertaken by Monica Charlot.[14] Charlot sought to classify the positions of the Conservative and Labour parties on six internationally significant dimensions of political competition. On a left-right scale in which extreme differences would score 10, and domplete consensus zero, the two parties were on average 2.7 points apart in 1945 and even less in 1970, with Labour on average 0.8 to the left of centre and the Conservatives 0.8 to the right.

Three major issues that divide parties into Adversaries in many European countries are of little effect in Britain. On the relationship of Church and State, historically crucial in differentiating parties and voters throughout most of Europe, Conservative and Labour party manifestos are silent, because there has been no significant partisan controversy on religion in Britain since pre-1914 disputes about religion in education. On international security, there has been a vocal consensus between Conservative and Labour manifestos from 1945 to 1970, supporting British membership in the North Atlantic diplomatic and military alliance. By contrast, in France and Italy, the major parties are Adversaries in debates about how their country should be aligned internationally. The positive consensus is left-of-centre on a third issue: endorsement of the social security measures of the welfare state. While the Conservative and Labour parties differ about the extent and means of financing pensions, education and the health service, they agree on the principles of these welfare state measures, unlike, for example, Democrats and Republicans in America.

Differences between the party manifestos are consistently registered in three important economic fields: nationalization vs. free enterprise; the planned economy vs. the market economy; and the redistribution of

47

wealth vs. an acceptance of economic inequality. The redistribution of wealth differentiates the two parties consistently, but not as much as the ownership of industry. In an election document, Labour does not wish to emphasize that it might actually take money from millions, nor do Conservatives wish to emphasize that they favour maintaining the wealth of a small electoral minority. Planning the economy divides the two parties less consistently. From time to time the Conservatives view planning as "not unacceptable," and it is normally endorsed by the Labour manifesto. Differences on economic policy persist from election to election, according to Charlot, but they are not extreme, from 1945 to 1970 averaging 2.9 on a 10-point scale of differences on economic policy.[15]

At the constituency level, the election addresses of parliamentary candidates offer further evidence of where MPs and candidates stand on the major issues of the day. If candidates were opposing each other on the issues as well as in personal terms, then their addresses would concentrate on the same set of issues. In fact, this does not occur. A detailed examination of election addresses from 1950 through 1970 found that only two or three issues are mentioned by half the candidates in both parties at a given election.[16] Many of the frequently mentioned issues tend to be consensual; for example, there is nothing uniquely Conservative or Labour in opposing unemployment. It is unusual for a majority of candidates to mention an issue on which the two parties are adversaries, such as nationalization in 1950, nuclear weapons in 1959 and 1964, or education in 1970.

Typically, candidates compete by "talking past" each other. They do not stress different positions on the same issues, but different issues. In 1979, 88 percent of Conservative candidates stressed the issue of tax cuts and 87 percent mentioned law and order, more than twice the mentions by Labour candidates. The reticence of Labour and the vociferousness of Conservatives reflected the fact that the Labour government was not reckoned to have handled these issues well. Similarly, 82 percent of Labour candidates mentioned pensions, 79 percent paybeds in NHS hospitals and 50 percent child benefits, all fields in which Labour was particularly interested, more than twice the proportion of Conservatives referring to these issues.[17] Parliamentary candidates tend to talk past each other in order to concentrate on what they see as their own strong points.

In the media-oriented national campaign, party leaders appeal to voters to make a choice. But the speeches of the party leaders are not so much a debate about policy as they are an attempt to resolve a general question of competence. Each side devotes more effort to attacking the competence of its opponents than to establishing the credibility of its policies for governing the country in future.

In the 1970 general election, the then Prime Minister, Harold Wilson, devoted 75 percent of his major speeches to attacking the Conservatives and only 20 percent to defending the record of the 1964–70 Labour government, and 5 percent to future policies. The leader of the opposition, Edward Heath, devoted 70 percent of his time to criticizing the actions of the Labour government, consistent with the idea that the opposition's task is to oppose; another 30 percent was devoted to a positive outline of Conservative policies (see table 3.7). In the peculiar circumstances of the February 1974 election campaign, the Prime Minister, Edward Heath, devoted 47 percent of his speeches to defending the government's policies—but he devoted almost as much (36 percent) to attacking the shortcomings of the opposition. In opposition, as in office, Harold Wilson spent much more time discussing the Conservatives' shortcomings than in expounding Labour policies. Impressionistically, the 1979 election campaign appears to have been as negative as the 1970 contest. James Callaghan seemed readier to attack the putative policies of the opposition than to defend the record of his own government, which the Conservatives took delight in calling to the attention of the electorate.

If the rhetoric of party leaders is to be believed, a British general election does offer a choice, but it is an ironic choice—between the Devil the Deep Blue Sea, or, as one politician reading this manuscript commented, "Between the Devil you know and the Devil you don't know." Insofar as each leader attacks the other, the electorate is told who *not* to

TABLE 3.7 *Positive and Negative Rhetoric in the Speeches of Party Leaders, 1970–74*

	1970 Election		February 1974 Election	
	Heath %	Wilson %	Heath %	Wilson %
Attacking other side	70	75	36	69
Defending own record	na	20	47	8
Expounding future policies	30	5	17	23

SOURCES: David Robertson, "The Content of Election Addresses and Leaders' Speeches," in *The British General Election of 1970*, ed. D. E. Butler and Michael Pinto-Duschinsky (London: Macmillan, 1971), pp. 442–45; Shelley Pinto-Duschinsky, "A Matter of Words," *New Society*, 7 March 1974.

vote for. The electorate cannot gain a clear idea of the positive difference between the parties if the Prime Minister does not wish to defend his party's record in government, and the leader of the opposition is disinclined to expound an alternative set of policies.

Symbols and phrases in the speeches of the two party leaders show that they are less "political" in the Adversary sense than might be inferred from table 3.7. During February 1974, both party leaders avoided reference to ideologically distinctive party themes. Edward Heath did not talk about a "great divide" between the parties, but rather emphasized "fairness" above all else in his speeches. There were only five mentions of free enterprise themes in Heath's major speeches. The leader of the Labour Party, Harold Wilson, mentioned Socialism only twice in the campaign, once when speaking from a platform draped with a Union Jack and the traditional Conservative slogan "One Nation."[18]

The favoured words of the party leaders in the crisis election of February 1974 were lacking party political implications. Edward Heath talked about fairness, strength, moderation and responsibility, and Harold Wilson spoke about his concern for families, the British people and housewives, and his anxieties about political crisis and divisiveness. While each leader could give these words distinctive partisan nuances, the overall effect was to emphasize consensual values. Edward Heath could be for families and against crisis, just as Harold Wilson could endorse fairness, moderation and national strength. Such consensus has liabilities, as Michael Pinto-Duschinsky noted in a review of the year's campaigning in 1974:

> The vagueness of the language of national unity excuses the three (i.e. including the Liberal) party leaders from awkward discussions as to precisely how they propose to tackle the country's problems.[19]

Overall, the test of elections tends to uphold the Consensus rather than the Adversary model of party politics. Voters do differ in their choice of parties, but they are not ranged against each other in opposing classes. Electoral competition in Britain produces divisions cutting across class lines. Moreover, on many important policies there is a Consensus view within the electorate; a majority of voters in both parties agree about what they would like the government to do. Many of the most noteworthy differences of political opinion are *within* the ranks of the Labour voters and within the Labour leadership as well.

The logic of electoral competition requires that parties differentiate themselves in some way. But they do not do this by Adversary confrontation. Instead, the parties issue manifestos that are anodyne in outward appearance, and even on major economic issues their differences have tended to be limited. In campaign appeals to the electorate, constituency candidates and, even more, party leaders, tend to avoid confrontation on issues. The differences the parties stress are few but, in their minds, all important. First and foremost, the parties disagree about which team of politicians is best suited to carry out the broadly consensual wishes of the electorate.

CHAPTER 4

Testing the Manifesto

Elections are occasional; government is continuous. The Manifesto model takes a long view of party politics. It is concerned not so much with the outcome of a brief election campaign as it is with what happens before and what happens after, especially when the opposition becomes the government. The Manifesto model takes a positive view of the policy-making role of parties. It asserts that a party newly elected to office will use the power gained to redeem the pledges and hopes that it raised in opposition.

Election manifestos are a hinge turning generalized political values and ideas into statements of particular intentions to act. Political ideologies are abstract. A political ideology must be vague in parts, meaning many things in different circumstances, if it is to survive as an idealized and relatively timeless statement of how a country should be governed. But government is concrete. The record of government is not what an ideology prescribes as ideal; it is what a government does in particular and often difficult circumstances.

To translate a political philosophy into practice requires a party to specify a substantial number of specific measures that it can implement during the lifetime of a Parliament. A government will also be forced to act in response to unforeseen (and often undesirable) events. But to give positive direction to government, it must also have policies that deal with relatively prosaic matters. Just as an architect's blueprint is only realized by laying down building blocks and by work not visible to the eye, so a party wishing to influence society must do so by identifying specific programmes that can influence society in detail.

Manifestos are controversial documents; both politicians and students of politics disagree about what they do and should contain. Politicians strongly committed to a particular design for society believe that manifestos should follow the Adversary model of party politics, offering

the nation a clear choice between alternative ways of life. There is disagreement within both parties about whether manifestos do offer voters
a big enough choice. Electorally oriented politicians tend to view manifestos as Consensus documents; they do not wish to make adversaries of
any group of voters deemed necessary to win an election. In the preparation of a manifesto, politicians can disagree about what ought to go in
it, according to the emphasis they give to party principles as against electoral tactics. In 1979 the controversy was dramatically demonstrated
when the draft manifesto prepared by the National Executive Committee
of the Labour Party was rejected by a Labour Prime Minister who considered it electorally harmful.

The purpose of this chapter is to test whether a party in government
acts upon the intentions set out in the manifesto it prepares in opposition.
The first section analyzes the growing significance of the manifesto to
both political parties. The second section compares what parties say in
their manifestos, and what happens to these pledges when a party wins
the power to carry them out. The concluding section considers whether
the manifestos better fit the Adversary or Consensus model of party
politics.

The Evolution of the Manifesto

In the language of generalities that constitutes writings about the British
Constitution, a newly elected government is said to have a mandate to
govern. However, as Professor Wilfrid Harrison has noted, "It is always
far from clear from the mere election result just what any government's
mandate is."[1] A governing party could use the mandate doctrine to justify
carrying out any measure it chooses, but the less popular its policies are,
the more controversy this creates. If the governing party can demonstrate
that the measures it is taking were contained in its election manifesto, it
can use this to justify the claim that the electorate has given a mandate for
what is being done.

The doctrine of the mandate implies a contract between the governing party and the voters, but the metaphor of a contract is misleading
in several respects. First, the electorate is not organized to "instruct" any
party what it wants done, as an individual or an organization might instruct a lawyer to draw up a contract to carry out its wishes. Instead, the
initiative rests with the party to prepare the manifesto for which it claims
a mandate. The electorate cannot exercise a veto on particular items in a

manifesto, even though a substantial portion may disagree with many party policies contained in every manifesto (cf. table 3.3). Second, the statements that parties make in their election manifestos need not be precise or comprehensive, like a legal document. There is no means to enforce a mandate if a government evades its commitments, nor is there any way to prevent a government acting outside the bounds of its manifesto. The power to determine what an election mandate is worth rests with the governing party and not with the voters who give it. The ultimate recourse of the electorate is to turn the governing party out of office, but by doing so it seems to give a mandate to its opponents.

While the first recognized party manifesto was issued by Sir Robert Peel at Tamworth in 1834, the manifesto has only recently assumed its contemporary importance.[2] At the turn of the century, party manifestos were brief exhortations to voters, not detailed programmes. In 1900, the Conservatives won office with a manifesto that made only two general commitments: to maintain the Imperial Power in South Africa, and to strengthen the nation's military force. In 1906, the Liberal manifesto concentrated on attacking the Conservatives. The one positive Liberal commitment — to free trade — was voiced incidentally in an attack on the Conservative threat to introduce tariffs, or as Mr. Balfour's manifesto described it, "reform our fiscal system." The Liberal manifesto gave no hint of what was to be done by one of the major innovating governments of this century. Sir Henry Campbell-Bannerman simply stated, "Our own policy is well known to you and I need not here repeat the terms."[3]

In the course of three-quarters of a century, election manifestos have grown in tandem with the growth of government. Labour launched its first election campaign with an eighteen-line manifesto. The Conservatives won the 1900 election with a manifesto of two pages. Up to the outbreak of the 1914 war, the manifestos of the leading parties averaged less than three pages. Between the wars, manifestos averaged little less than four pages. In elections from 1945 to 1959, manifestos doubled in length to an average of nearly nine pages. Party manifestos have doubled again in size since 1964, as both the Labour and Conservative parties have devoted more and more attention to setting policies before the electorate. The enunciation of policies is not the prerogative of Socialist planners. Throughout the century, Conservative Party manifestos have usually been longer than the statements of their Labour opponents.

As election manifestos have become longer, they have become increasingly specific in content, containing more and more statements about what a party intends to do in office. More detailed discussion of policies also reflects a declining belief in the general utility of single principles, whether "Socialism," "Free Trade" or "Empire." Sentiments, symbols and scarifying criticisms of opponents are inadequate to give guidance to contemporary government.

TABLE 4.1   *The Growing Length of Election Manifestos, 1900–1979*

	Conservative	Labour	Liberal	Average, Two Leading Parties
	(average page length)			
1900–1910	2.0	0.5	3.7	2.8
1922–35	4.7	3.2	2.5	3.9
1945–59	11.0	6.5	4.5	8.7
1964–74	19.5	18.5	10.0	19.0
1979	14.5	17.0	13.2	15.7

SOURCE: F. W. S. Craig, *British General Election Manifestos, 1900–1974* (London: Macmillan, 1975); and *The Times Guide to the House of Commons* (London: Times Books, 1979), adjusted to allow for differences in words per page.

The prominence given manifestos today has revealed limitations. Professor S. E. Finer attacks parties for deceiving themselves, the electorate or both with "Manifesto moonshine."[4] Manifestos are perceived as Adversary documents, and the country suffers from "too much" Adversary politics, because the governing party treats its manifesto as a mandate for action. Finer argues that a manifesto cannot be a valid mandate for fifty or a hundred Acts of Parliament, for voters do not read, let alone think about, so wide a range of issues when casting their ballot. Once in office, a party finds itself committed to policies that careful examination in Whitehall shows to be impracticable or undesirable. Equally important, changing circumstances may make it impossible or unwise to pursue some objectives. Finer concludes:

> Shopping-list type manifestos simultaneously do too much and too little. When a government sets out to be "faithful," it is frequently unwise; and when it has learned to be wise, it is frequently unfaithful.[5]

Whereas Finer attacks "manifesto-itis" because he believes that a party in office pays too much attention to what it said in opposition, Professor Anthony King criticizes manifestos for the opposite reason. King alleges that a voter reading a party's manifesto cannot predict what the party will do in office. Manifestos are dismissed as empty and meaningless documents having a "virtually random" relationship to what a party will do in office, because there is said to be an almost total "lack of fit" between the world as manifesto writers see it and the world as it really is.[6]

Whether professors like it or not, British parties devote a considerable amount of time, talk and, at times, acrimonious debate to the preparation of election manifestos. This is as true of the Conservative Party, with its dozens of committees working away quietly and often anonymously under the auspices of the Conservative Research Department, as it is of Labour, where Transport House could boast that from 1974 to 1979 it had produced 70 "major" NEC statements, a 60,000-word 1976 programme, and commissioned more than 2,000 research papers.[7]

A party's manifesto is immediately important as an exercise in party management. Even though few ordinary voters will read the document, it is sure to be read and read closely by politicians asked to endorse its authoritative statement of the party's policy intentions. Moreover, parliamentary candidates read their party's manifesto carefully for guidance about what they ought to say, and equally, for warnings about the limits to promises for which the party can collectively be held responsible.[8] Given the diversity of opinions within each of the two major parties, the drafting of a manifesto is first of all a search for consensus *within* each of the parties. The resulting document is not so much a statement of what the voters want as it is a proclamation of what a party's leadership agrees to want.

Government and opposition face in opposite directions when thinking about manifestos. The governing party is concerned with carrying out (or evading) the commitments in its past manifesto. Some may be enacted easily, but others are sure to cause difficulty. If ministers are tempted to forget the more awkward of their manifesto pledges, their own or opposition MPs are sure to provide reminders. Leaders of the party in power have little time to think about preparing a manifesto for the next election; they are busy determining what the present Parliament will do. The party "outside the gates" of Whitehall may loyally support what the government does or, if this is unpopular, adopt an alternative approach to policy making, one which takes advantage of distance from office to concentrate on thinking in terms of good (or ideologically congenial) intentions.

The first instinct of a party entering opposition is to defend its record in office; the motive for doing so is strongest in the party leader, now an ex-Prime Minister. But many colleagues will wish to think again about policies that have gone down in defeat. Moreover, the act of electoral defeat will force the leadership into admitting that "something" has gone wrong. Dissatisfaction with the election defeat will encourage the opposition to talk about future policies. As ex-ministers retire or change their interests, new voices will be heard in party conclaves, declaiming what the party ought to do when next in power. Free from the responsibilities of office, the opposition can attack unpopular policies of the present government and say what the party would like to happen if it is returned to office at the next general election. In deciding what is "likeable," an opposition usually does not turn to opinion polls to learn what promises might be generally popular. It turns to its most articulate leaders to see what they commend as desirable. The results of opposition deliberations are thus fundamentally defective, argues King, because opposition leaders believe that the willpower sufficient to formulate policy intentions is also sufficient to make a difference to what government does. King charges that politicians "suffer from hubris—the belief that, if only *they* were in power, things would be different. Oppositions dwell in a house not of power but of words."[9]

The preparation of the manifestos presents a common problem to which the Conservative and Labour parties respond differently. Contrary to what might be expected, the Conservative Party should be better able to carry out its manifesto intentions than the Labour Party. This is because the parliamentary party, and above all the parliamentary leader, determine the contents of a Conservative manifesto. Nothing need be included that goes against the wishes of the party's parliamentary leaders, and they have every incentive to fill the manifesto with policies that they believe to be both popular and practicable.

A Conservative manifesto is not a personal statement. It is the product of a committee carefully constituted to reflect different outlooks within the party, and different institutions within the party. There can be no clash between the views of Conservatives at Westminster and the extraparliamentary party because, in the frank words of one of the officers of the National Union of Conservative & Unionist Associations, the latter has "no effect whatsoever on party policy."[10]

The specific procedures for preparing Conservative manifestos have varied considerably with the character of the leader.[11] Winston Churchill and, latterly Anthony Eden, were prepared to delegate the work of preparing manifestos to R. A. Butler, as Chairman of the Conservative Research Department. Butler was less concerned with the details of policy than with "broadbrush" statements of political values intended to create the impression of the Conservatives as a party in tune with the outlook of postwar Britain. Shortly after becoming Conservative Prime Minister, Harold Macmillan established and chaired a Steering Committee on party policy that met seventeen times between December 1957 and the 1959 general election. Macmillan gave careful attention to proposals for the manifesto. Occasionally he would interrupt discussions of future policy by enquiring: "What's the point of waiting? Why not do it now?" Elected as leader in opposition in 1965, Edward Heath took personal charge of the development of policies for the 1970 general election manifesto.

After Margaret Thatcher assumed office in opposition in 1975, she sought to stamp her imprint on Conservative policy, but was not in a strong position to resolve intraparty disputes about policy. In reaction against Heath's style, she was less concerned with preparing policies in detail than with the broad direction and tone of policy. Her foreword to the 1979 manifesto selected five principal themes. But the institutionalization of manifesto pledges is so great that the manifesto itself contained upwards of one hundred specific policy pledges under forty-one different headings, ranging from defence (five specific pledges to strengthen defence by spending more money) to animal welfare (five specific pledges to alter regulations concerning the living conditions of farm animals, the use of live animals in experiments and the transportation of animals for sale and slaughter). Moreover, five months after the party entered office the Conservative Research Department was cataloguing under eighteen different headings how "The Conservative government has already implemented many election pledges."[12]

The Labour Party, by contrast, is dualistic in direction: both the party in Parliament and the extraparliamentary party claim a voice in making policy.[13] The party's 1918 Constitution (Clause V.1) lays down that the party's programme should be determined by a two-thirds majority vote of Annual Conference. The Parliamentary Labour Party is charged by the Constitution (Clause IV.3) with the object: "To give effect as far as may be practicable to the principles from time to time approved by the Party Conference." Clause V.2 of the Constitution has held that it is the joint responsibility of the National Executive Committee and the Parliamentary Labour Party to decide "which items from the Party Programme shall be included in the Manifesto." Within the party, the manifesto can be viewed as a "contract" between the two different parts of the party, registering the extent to which MPs and ministers are committed to Conference decisions within the lifetime of a Labour government. Given two different centres of policy making in the party—one oriented to Westminster and the national electorate, and the other to the Party Conference—inevitably there are difficulties in determining what policies "may be practicable" for a government to put into effect.

In the 1945–51 Labour government, the internal party controversy was limited by the success of the Attlee administration in adopting and implementing much welfare state legislation, and by the backing that trade unions gave the government when it was challenged by left-wing groups. From 1951 to 1964 internal party disputes did not concern government. The major disputes were about "domestic" foreign policy, that is, the opposition's view of what the government ought to do about German rearmament and nuclear disarmament. The parliamentary leadership won these disputes, but it had to "fight, fight and fight again" to outmanoeuvre its opponents.

The return of a Labour government in 1964 gave dominance to Labour's parliamentary leadership, which immediately decided government policy. The 1970 Labour election manifesto did not result in a conflict between the two decision-making centres of the party, because it was prepared in a preelection atmosphere of "comfortable complacent euphoria" in which any suggestion for including a policy in the manifesto that deviated from the government's course "was resisted on the grounds that it implied that the Minister concerned had not been doing as well as he should."[14] Had a conflict arisen, the NEC would have been defeated for, as the parliamentary party chairman Douglas Houghton told the final meeting about the manifesto with the NEC: "Look, if the government doesn't want to carry out any of your promises, it won't."[15]

During the 1970s the split between the two parts of the Labour Party widened further. *Labour's Programme 1973* contained many statements to the left of the previous government—but many of these were not found in the 1974 Labour manifestos. During the 1974–79 Labour government, the dual structure split. The NEC again and again publicly attacked policies of the Labour government. It issued *Labour's Programme 1976*, a 147-page document intended to serve as the basis for policies of the next Labour government.[16] The present Labour government ignored policy commitments of the party's Annual Conference. Transport House staff admitted there was some justification:

> Sometimes the commitment turned out to be too vague or unclear; sometimes Ministers preferred to interpret the commitment in their own way because of a basic lack of sympathy on their part with the proposal itself;

or sometimes, it was found that the commitment had not been properly thought through.[17]

While the 1974–1979 Labour government was busy carrying out its *current* policies, the NEC prepared to work out "a programme of action, clear and unambiguous, for the *next* government."[18] When the two met to agree a manifesto for the 1979 general election, the differences between the more adversary NEC document and the government proposals were regarded as "appalling" by the chief NEC staff participant. The Prime Minister twice threatened to resign if the NEC's version was adopted as the campaign manifesto, so much did he disagree with its contents. In the event, the party of Downing Street defeated the Transport House part of the Labour Party. The National Executive Committee found, in the words of its Research Secretary, that it was

> ... a mere pressure group, just one among many. The outcome of our numerous delegations, representations, statements and resolutions was thus little different from those of many other pressure groups: a few minor successes, perhaps, but little of real substance in the way of changing the direction of Government policy.[19]

In opposition, the balance of power has shifted again. The October 1979 Labour Party Conference voted to make the NEC solely responsible for preparing the party's manifesto, a policy that James Callaghan, as leader of the parliamentary party, has staunchly opposed. But before the Conference decision can determine the course of British government, three conditions must be met. The NEC must dictate the contents of Labour's next election manifesto, overriding such objections as are voiced by the parliamentary party. Second, the Labour Party must win the election fought on such a manifesto. Third, the resulting Labour government must implement the proposals contained in the NEC document.

Even though few politicians expect to implement all their manifesto pledges, most politicians believe that their party manifesto is important in "putting down a marker" about their intentions for government.[20] From a committed partisan's perspective, the greater the pressures for a party in office to carry on with the policies of its predecessor, the greater the case for committing it to an Adversary stance while in opposition. The manifesto signifies to party activists what it would like to do. It warns opponents that they will have no constitutional justification to prevent the adoption of controversial policies that have been put before the electorate beforehand. The manifesto also serves notice on civil servants of measures that Whitehall should consider primary political commitments of a newly elected government. Civil servants complaining about the wisdom of adopting a policy may be intimidated with the declaration: "It's in the party manifesto."

A manifesto is not a statement of what a party will achieve in practice but of what it intends to achieve. It is not an immutable contract entered into between voters and party leaders. Voters have no way to bind those they elect to do what they wish. Nor can politicians in office compel events to produce what they promised when in opposition. Once in office, the manifesto is a touchstone by which the current practice of the governing party can be assessed; it can also be an albatross signifying that its achievements are wanting.

What Is Said and What Is Done

An election manifesto is, first, a piece of political journalism; its purpose is to persuade, and to do so by evoking partisan slogans and symbols. For example, the 1970 Conservative manifesto starts by denouncing the Labour government for its "bad policies," and for its "cheap and trivial style of government." The Conservatives promised to "re-establish our sound and honest British traditions." The February 1974 Labour manifesto commenced by denouncing the Conservative government for calling "this election in panic; they are unable to govern and dare not tell the people the truth." It blamed the Conservatives for the nation's "most serious political and economic crisis since 1945" and pledged to provide "a government of all the people."

But a modern election manifesto has become an example of quality journalism. Whereas a *Mirror* or *Express* editorial of a few hundred words can be confined to invective and glittering generalities, a party manifesto of up to ten thousand words must identify specific problems, and give some indication of what the party would like to do, if it is to carry conviction. Beneath sloganeering headlines, a contemporary election manifesto contains much fine print detailing specific intentions to act. This is important, because much of what a party can do in office is concerned with the fine print of government.

The opportunity for a party to translate manifesto intentions into government policy is surprisingly infrequent. In the seven Parliaments from 1955 to 1979, there is only one example of an opposition preparing plans that it is immediately able to act upon after a general election: the Conservative entry to office with a secure majority in 1970, following a full Parliament preparing for office. By contrast, Harold Macmillan and

Sir Alec Douglas-Home each inherited the ongoing commitments of an established government upon becoming Prime Minister. The 1959 Conservative Party manifesto is not a good test of the significance of a manifesto, for inevitably it was influenced by the tendency of a governing party to adjust its electoral commitments to its experience of office. The Labour Party has twice moved from opposition to government in the past three decades, but on both occasions was initially handicapped by the lack of a satisfactory majority, and had to fight a second general election to confirm its position. The 1974–79 period of Labour government is here chosen for comparison with the Conservative government under Edward Heath. Because there was so little distance between the 1974 elections, the two 1974 Labour manifestos are treated as a single document.[21]

In 1970 and 1974, the opposition entering office was led by an experienced politician with ample prior experience of the difficulties and opportunities of office. Each party had been sufficiently long in opposition to prepare for the day when it could propose rather than oppose government policy, and each then had time enough in office to test whether manifesto commitments were guides to action.

The first task in analyzing a manifesto is to separate the wheat from the chaff, that is, to identify specific pledges that can then be tested to see whether or not they were achieved. The tables that follow disregard manifesto statements that are so vague or general that it is impossible to tell, after the event, whether or not they have been accomplished. For example, if a party says it will "do our best for the nation's troubled economy," this is disregarded because no indication is given of what would happen if the party did do its best. The line between a vague statement and a verifiable pledge is easily overlooked by the rapid reader. It is a constant concern of manifesto authors, who always have the option of "fudging" the party's intentions rather than giving a specific pledge.

Both the Conservative and Labour manifestos are full of dozens of specific statements of policy intentions (see table 4.2). In 1970 the Conservative Party offered 96 specific pledges and in the two 1974 elections, 126. Labour too gave many manifesto hostages to fortune: 83 in 1970 and 104 in 1974. The difference between the parties is not so much in the number of pledges as it is in their fate. There was never any opportunity to learn what Labour would have done to carry out its 1970 manifesto, or how the Conservatives would have carried out their 1974 manifestos, for in each case the party lost the election.

Nearly one-third of all manifesto pledges concerned the most immediate problem facing Britain in the 1970s, the economy. Problems of

TABLE 4.2   *The Number and Subject of Manifesto Pledges, 1970–74*

	Conservatives 1970		Labour 1970		Labour 1974		Conservatives 1974		Total
	N	%	N	%	N	%	N	%	%
The Economy (Treasury, Trade, Industry, Employment)	30	31	24	29	39	37	32	25	30
Environment	15	16	21	25	18	17	29	23	20
Home Office and Parliamentary	15	16	13	16	12	12	22	17	15
Health and Social Security	20	21	6	7	15	14	15	12	14
Education and Science	7	7	9	11	10	10	20	16	11
Foreign Affairs and Defence	6	6	10	12	8	7	4	3	7
Agriculture	3	3	0	0	3	3	4	3	2
	96	100%	83	100%	105	100%	126	100%	99%

SOURCE: Manifestos as printed in F. W. S. Craig, *British General Election Manifestos 1900–1974* (London: Macmillan, 1975), pp. 325–44, 398–406, 451–67.

the Department of Environment, such as housing and local government matters, ranked second in frequency, providing one-fifth of the manifesto pledges. The major services of the Welfare State—health, social security and education—together received one-quarter of all mentions. Interestingly, in both 1970 and 1974, the Conservatives were readier to refer to such issues than was Labour, showing that they did not believe that the Labour Party "owned" these issues. Reciprocally, Labour was readier to pronounce on foreign affairs and defence than the Conservatives, even though the latter is traditionally more closely identified with foreign affairs.

The number and variety of manifesto pledges made by the two parties are realistic in governmental terms, even though too numerous for popular discussion during an election campaign. To carry out a manifesto, a party would need to act on 20 to 25 pledges per session of Parliament. This is less than half the number of bills actually enacted in a session, and many pledges can be met without legislation by the exercise of administrative discretion, or by shifting public expenditure. No single Cabinet minister could claim that the commitments in his party's manifesto were impossibly numerous. A manifesto sets down an average of up to six markers per department for attainment in a five-year period of government.

A second important feature of manifesto pledges is whether they specify measures that government can take or point towards goals without specific means to desired ends. For example, a pledge to alter public spending for a given programme or to introduce a law regulating the payment of social security benefit is "do-able," for government has the legal powers to undertake such actions. By contrast, a pledge to reduce the rate of inflation is a promise without any indication of how (or whether) the government can do this. The more a party concentrates on pledging actions that government *can* take, the more realistic its manifesto is. The more it concentrates on pledging achievements that it would wish to realize, without specifying its means, the more its manifesto is a statement of aspirations rather than a guide to action.

In practice, both the Conservative and Labour party manifestos concentrate on "do-able" pledges, that is, actions immediately within the control of government. When the Conservatives entered office in 1970, 75 percent of their pledges concerned measures directly within the control of government; and 82 percent of Labour's 1974 pledges concerned actions in the hands of government. When faced with the biggest problem of all—the management of the economy—both parties are realistic about what they can do. The 1970 Conservative manifesto concentrated on twenty-two measures a government could take, such as repealing the selective employment tax and introducing a value-added tax. Similarly, the 1974 Labour manifesto contained thirty-four specific pledges of action within the power of Parliament, such as establishing a National Enterprise Board and buying shares in companies. It was exceptional for parties to state intentions as vague as promising to "improve local social services" (Conservatives, 1970) or "transform the area health authorities into democratic bodies" (Labour, 1974). In short, parties enumerate what they *can* do; they do not treat the writing of a manifesto as if it were writing a letter to Santa Claus.

The readiness of British parties to proclaim dozens of specific policy intentions and to cast them in "do-able" terms subjects the manifesto of the governing party to a hard and practical test. A party that carried out its intentions would, by following the Manifesto model, uphold its "contract" with the electorate. The results might be displeasing to some voters, but they could not complain that they had not been told what the government was going to do. By contrast, a governing party that ignored its manifesto intentions would indicate that it regarded opposition as a period for *not* thinking seriously about public policy.

TABLE 4.3   *How Parties Act upon Their Manifestos, 1970–79*

	Conservative Government 1970–74				Labour Government 1974–79			
	Acted upon	Ambig-uous	No Action	Oppo-site	Acted upon	Ambig-uous	No Action	Oppo-site
The Economy	22	2	5	1	26	4	9	0
Environment	13	1	1	0	8	4	5	1
Home Office and Parliamentary	11	3	1	0	5	2	5	0
Health and Social Security	17	2	1	0	10	4	1	0
Education and Science	7	0	0	0	2	3	5	0
Foreign Affairs and Defence	5	1	0	0	3	3	2	0
Agriculture	2	1	0	0	3	0	0	0
Totals	77	10	8	1	57	20	27	1
	(80%)	(10%)	(8%)	(1%)	(54%)	(19%)	(26%)	(1%)

SOURCE: As in table 4.2.

Both the Conservative and Labour governments act consistently with the Manifesto model of governing; in office they do the majority of things to which they pledge themselves in their opposition manifestos. The 1970–74 Heath government fulfilled at least 80 percent of its manifesto pledges, and showed some evidence of action in another 10 percent of cases. Faced with a very difficult parliamentary situation in which it often could not be sure of a majority, the 1974–79 Labour government nonetheless acted unambiguously upon 54 percent of all its manifesto commitments and gave some evidence of action upon another 19 percent (see table 4.3). Notwithstanding caustic comments about particular U-turns of the Heath administration and the Labour government's reversal on incomes policy, the great bulk of the manifesto commitments of both parties—up to 90 percent in the Conservative case and up to 73 percent in the case of Labour—were in fact acted upon.

The evidence of table 4.3 is in accord with the boasts that each party made to its supporters about the fulfillment of manifesto pledges. In 1974 Conservative Central Office claimed that the Heath government had made 105 manifesto pledges and implemented 97 of them. The high success rate in the Conservative account reflected a generous interpretation of evidence. For example, the Conservatives claimed that their 1973 National Health Service Reorganization Act had improved the coordination of the health services—though by 1979, the party manifesto claimed that it wished to "decentralize the service and cut back bureaucracy."

In 1979, *Labour Weekly*, published at Transport House, enumerated 69 pledges from the party's October 1974 manifesto and announced that the Labour government had carried out 52 of them in whole or substantial part, commenced work on another 8 measures, and made no progress on 9 policies covered in the manifesto. *Labour Weekly*'s high success rate also reflects a generous interpretation of evidence. For example, it counted a pledge to "improve road safety" carried out because the Ministry had "doubled the advertising budget for road safety."[22]

Parties rarely act in complete contradiction to their manifesto pledges. The few occasions when this has happened are noteworthy because of the substantive importance of particular issues, for example, the Heath government's so-called U-turn on statutory wage controls, and the Wilson government's cut in local authority mortgage lending in 1975–76, after promising to expand it in its 1974 manifesto. One reason why contradictions are few is that British parties have a sense of commitment to policy intentions. A second reason is that when circumstances are expected to prove difficult, the manifesto can be drafted with a loophole. This gives a subsequent government an excuse for acting in a manner that surprises but does not explicitly contradict the party's commitments. For example, when the Conservatives wrote into their 1970 manifesto that they were "totally opposed to further nationalisation of British industry," this statement was followed by the comment that "specific projects approved by Parliament will continue to be given government support." Hence, when Rolls-Royce was nationalized by Act of Parliament in 1971, this was claimed to be within the letter (if not the spirit) of the manifesto.[23]

Inaction is the usual explanation for a manifesto pledge not being realized. For example, although the Heath government usually acted positively, it did not enact pledged legislation to require disclosure of more information about the accounts of public companies. The 1974–79

Labour government had a harder task in implementing manifesto pledges because of financial constraints resulting from the world economic recession. Whereas the Conservatives could pledge to raise the school leaving age to sixteen and did so in 1972, Labour was unable to find the money to carry out such important party commitments as phasing out prescription charges. Nor did it try to impose upon employers the cost of financing compulsory paid day release for young workers. Moreover, Labour's lack of a secure parliamentary majority meant that any measure that might unite *all* its non-Socialist opponents in opposition was very risky. The Labour government was unable to nationalize ship-repairing, nor did it introduce a wealth tax. But these omissions are the exception not the rule. For the most part, British parties do in office what they propose in opposition.

If manifestos are to be criticized, it is because they may concentrate too much on things that government can do—enacting legislation, appointing committees of inquiry and marginally altering spending on particular programmes. From a ministerial perspective, these actions are important because they are what a government can do. From the perspective of citizens, government actions are but means to larger ends. The appointment of a committee of inquiry, or even the enactment of a bill, can carry out an intention stated in a manifesto and be a means to a further end. But there is no assurance that the chosen government's means will be sufficient to achieve desired social ends.

The gap between what government can do and what the public (and, for that matter, the government) wants to achieve is greatest in the management of the economy (see chap. 7). Successive governments offer the electorate realistically "do-able" statements of economic intent and, when elected, fulfill most of their pledges. Unfortunately, these small-scale "do-able" policies do not produce the economic benefits that appear to lie beyond the reach of either party. Voters are less impressed with realized intentions than they are depressed about unrealized goals.

Are Manifestos Adversary or Consensus Documents?

The fact that parties present manifestos that are "do-able" and usually carry out their intentions in office supports the Manifesto model of party government. But it does not confirm the Adversary model of party government as well. Chapter 3 has documented how anodyne are the titles that parties give manifestos, and the consensual nature of the campaigns of which the manifestos are a part. Logically, both the Manifesto model and the Consensus model of government could be true, if the measures promised and carried out by a party were also promised by its opponents, or at least were "not unacceptable" when presented to Parliament.

In election manifestos, parties are not so much contradicting each other as "talking past" each other. A systematic comparison of Conservative and Labour manifestos at the 1970 election found that with 86 percent of the topics raised, the parties were talking past each other, that is, raising different points for action by a given government department. In 1974, 86 percent of all issues raised in the manifestos avoided direct contradiction. Only one-seventh of the subjects discussed showed the two parties joining issue with each other. Party manifestos are not so much in conflict about how to resolve commonly perceived problems as they are statements of differing priorities for government action.[24]

Party manifestos concentrate on the same broad areas of political concern that are effectively fixed by the ongoing concerns of Whitehall departments and the major issues of the moment. However, the specific pledges that the parties make usually differ, without contradicting each other. For example, on education, the 1974 Conservative manifestos promised to strengthen the school inspectorate, insist on parents' representatives on school governing bodies, scrutinize zoning arrangements, oblige schools to have Parent Teacher Associations, and encourage school prospectuses. None of these questions was mentioned by Labour, and none was particularly controversial; they simply reflected Conservative perspectives and priorities for educational policy. Similarly, Labour promised to expand facilities for 16–18 year olds, institute compulsory day release for further education, and legislate for an annual report to Parliament on youth services, reflecting its own distinctive but not particularly controversial priorities.

Parties that talk past each other can still be Adversaries if the priorities that each enunciate are distinctively partisan. For example, if the Conservatives pledge encouragement for private health care, Labour can be expected to oppose this. Equally, if Labour pledges to strengthen trade union powers, it can expect Conservative opposition in Parliament to such a measure. Alternatively, parties can be consensual, albeit giving priority to different policies. For example, if one party pledges to improve nursery schools and the other to improve education for the mentally retarded, there is no reason to expect either party to oppose the other's proposal; in effect, each would be nonpartisan.

A systematic analysis of the 1970 and 1974 manifestos shows that slightly more than half (57 percent) of all manifestos pledges are nonpartisan (see table 4.4). The governing party is the more likely to make nonpartisan manifesto pledges. In 1970, 67 percent of Labour's manifesto pledges were nonpartisan, that is, unlikely to cause major divisions in the House of Commons. In 1974, 63 percent of the Conservative pledges were nonpartisan. As the challenger, the opposition is more likely to break consensus by putting forward partisan proposals. In 1970, 55 percent of the Conservative proposals were partisan, and in 1974, 52 percent of Labour's pledges. The difference is sufficient to suggest that the governing party normally wishes to contest an election as a Consensus party, whereas the opposition fears the status quo will be changed only if it breaks the Consensus by emphasizing that it offers an alternative to the policies of the governing party.

An opposition does not want to be excessively partisan, for that would reduce its potential electoral appeal. The point is particularly strong in the minds of Labour leaders. As James Callaghan explained to Kenneth Harris, the Labour Party should be "a broad Church," not a doctrinal sect. To make the point he suggested to his interviewer: "If you read our manifestos year after year, election after election, you will see how we have struck a balance that has carried the country forward."[25] A broad Church may make some doctrinal commitments—but it must also make nonpartisan proposals for change that are consensual, rather than expose the party to dividing a majority of the country against it.

TABLE 4.4   *Partisan and Nonpartisan Manifesto Pledges, 1970–74*

	Nonpartisan		Partisan	
	N	%	N	%
1970				
Conservatives	42	45	52	55
Labour	56	67	27	33
Totals	98	55	79	45
1974				
Conservatives	83	66	43	34
Labour	51	48	55	52
Totals	134	58	98	42

SOURCE: As in table 4.2.

When the opposition wins a general election and acts upon its manifesto pledges, it does increase the Adversary element in government. Systematic analysis of government legislation from 1970 to 1979 shows that the opposition divides against the government on second or third reading of 69 percent of the bills that are introduced in furtherance of manifesto pledges. The Conservative government is as ready as a Labour government to introduce controversial legislation pledged in its manifesto. The measures causing divisions include such specially controversial legislation as the Industrial Relations and the Housing Finance acts of the Heath government, and the repeal of the Industrial Relations Act by the subsequent Labour government.

The governing party's readiness to enact manifesto pledges does not, however, make the Commons an Adversary body. Only one-tenth of government legislation is based upon initiatives set out in party manifestos (see table 4.5). Many manifesto commitments can be met without specific legislation, such as increased spending on priority programmes or appointing an investigative or advisory committee.

The great bulk of governmental legislation is prepared independently of manifesto commitments. More than three-quarters of all the legislation that a government introduces is derived from the ongoing policy process in Whitehall. Whitehall departments continuously nag at

TABLE 4.5 *Legislative Initiatives and Consensus Responses, 1970–79*

	Consensus (no division)		Adversary (opposition division on 2nd/3rd readings)		Totals	
	N	%	N	%	N	%
1970–74						
Ongoing Whitehall process	120	84	23	16	143	81
Reaction to events	15	79	4	21	19	11
Manifesto initiative	5	33	10	67	15	8
Totals	140	79%	37	21%	177	100%
1974–79						
Ongoing Whitehall process	158	85	27	15	185	75
Reaction to events	22	79	6	21	28	11
Manifesto initiative	10	30	23	70	33	13
Totals	190	77%	56	23%	246	99%

SOURCE: As in table 4.2.

problems, whatever the colour of the party in office or the status of the parliamentary calendar. Civil servants consult with affected interests to see what can be done about problems of concern to departments and committees are appointed. Months or years later, the moving inertia of the Whitehall machine produces a recommendation for legislation. The party in power may have changed meanwhile, but the problems are still there. If the minister receives a report that all affected parties wish a new bill, he is likely to try to secure it as long as the proposal is not directly contradictory to received ideas in the governing party.

Manifesto commitments and Whitehall policies are both the result of deliberative processes working over a period of months or years. Whereas a manifesto pledge is discussed almost exclusively by partisans in opposition, a policy emerging from the ongoing Whitehall process is formulated by discussions with all affected groups, whatever their political inclinations. Therefore, legislation arising from Whitehall deliberations should normally be consensual and that arising from manifesto deliberations Adversary. This is in fact the case. Whereas two-thirds of manifesto bills cause major divisions in the Commons, five-sixths of bills derived from the Whitehall process are consensual, being enacted without a division in second or third reading in the House of Commons. There is no difference between the proportion of consensual generated by the Whitehall process under the 1970–74 Conservative government and the 1974–79 Labour government; in each case, five-sixths of such bills were consensual (see table 4.5).

Unexpected events—a foreign incident, an industrial emergency or the press disclosure of a scandal—sometimes force a governing party to react without the consensual advice of a departmental committee or the partisan guidance of a manifesto committee. In the 1970s, moreover, unexpected events have more often caused government legislation than have manifesto pledges (see table 4.5). Unexpected events might be expected to cause politicians to react by partisan instinct leading to Adversary confrontations in the Commons. Alternatively, it might be hypothesized that unexpected events would lead to Consensus, with partisan commitments set aside in the face of a national emergency.

Unexpected events lead to Consensus rather than Adversary legislation four-fifths of the time. This is true of the 1974–79 Labour government as well as the 1970–74 Conservative government (table 4.5). When unexpected events drive the governing party to act in accord with the opposition's wishes (e.g., the Heath government's nationalization of

Rolls-Royce to save jobs in 1971 and the Callaghan government's acceptance of tight money measures to secure an International Monetary Fund loan in 1976), dissent within the governing party may be more likely than an Adversary division. Even when this is not the case, the pressure of events is also a pressure for Consensus.

Examining the multiple sources of government legislation explains why action on manifesto pledges does not create Adversary government. It does not do so because these actions are a very small part of the total legislative activity of any government. In the 1970–74 Conservative government, only 8 percent of government bills can be attributed to the stimulus of the manifesto, and in the 1974–79 Labour government, 13 percent of bills. Nine-tenths of government legislation primarily reflects the ongoing policy process in Whitehall or the force of events. There are more divisions resulting from nonmanifesto measures than from manifesto measures. Only one-third of the divisions reported in table 4.5 concern bills arising from the party manifestos, and manifesto pledges cause Adversary divisions on only 7 percent of all government bills introduced in the House of Commons.

The evidence of the 1970s thus shows that party manifestos are important, but not in the way that is often alleged to be the case. Parties do make a large number of specific policy commitments in their manifestos, the commitments specify actions within the power of government and, once in office, both Conservative and Labour governments do carry out the majority of their commitments. In short, the evidence refutes the argument of Anthony King that government does nothing but make a series of U-turns away from "unrealistic" commitments.

Although party manifestos are important, they do not make British government Adversary government. The allegation of Professor Finer that manifestos *cause* divisions is itself "moonshine." Manifestos are not like a medieval disputation, with each party tenaciously asserting its own theses and refuting the heresies of its opponents. In the specific prescriptions put forward, parties tend to talk past each other. When manifesto pledges lead to legislation in the House of Commons, they are more likely to cause divisions than legislation derived from other sources, but manifesto legislation is only a very small proportion of the total legislation of a governing party. Moreover, many manifesto pledges can be implemented without legislation—and carried out consensually as well.[26]

As one turns to consider the totality of a government's policies rather than focusing solely upon what the manifesto said, the potential for

Consensus government increases greatly. Any party newly entering office will find many problems — and many responses — already at hand, reflecting the ongoing inertia processes of Whitehall. During its tenure of office, it will also be forced to react to circumstances that manifesto writers did not anticipate, or assumed should never occur. Manifesto pledges leave a mark on only one part of a government's total canvass of action. This can best be understood by examining government legislation, not in terms of what is laid down in a manifesto prepared in opposition, but in terms of what is recorded in the annals of Parliament.

CHAPTER 5

Adversary Parliament and Consensus Legislation

Laws are a unique resource of government. Whereas many institutions in society are able to raise money, hire personnel and organize on a large scale, only government has the power to enact laws determining what people can do. The party governing Britain does not determine every statute on the books. The laws of the land are an accretion of legislation passed by generations of government, and the great bulk of existing legislation is the subject of consensus between the parties. In the five-year life of a Parliament, however, the governing party can enact several hundred laws that will remain on the statute books long after it leaves office because of electoral defeat. It is the record of legislation that can make an enduring difference to society, whether passed by a Consensus or Adversary process.

The Adversary model of party government fits Parliament well. It is symbolized by the very architecture of the House of Commons: a pair of benches facing each other instead of a semicircle of deputies ranged around a Speaker's rostrum, as on the Continent or in the U.S. Congress. The styling of the largest party outside government as Her Majesty's Loyal Opposition gives official sanction to the doctrine that the opposition's job is to oppose. Debating procedures set partisans against each other, and climax in divisions in which each party is expected to muster its maximum numbers to vote on opposite sides of the question in dispute.

The opposition, not the government, is the party with the great vested interest in the Adversary model of party politics. Given Consensus, the party in office can claim that it is governing wisely and well. The opposition is made to appear redundant if it does not criticize the

74

government or claim that it would do things differently and better. The incentives of party politics encourage the opposition to exploit the procedures of Parliament to the full, in order to demonstrate its putative superiority to its Adversary.

By contrast, the governing party has an interest in minimizing parliamentary opposition to its actions, in order to claim that it is governing by Consensus. The incentives to do so go well beyond tactical party advantage. They arise from the desire of the majority party to make its actions acceptable (or "not unacceptable") to interest groups outside the House of Commons. Whereas the government can ride down opposition to legislation in the Commons by invoking its parliamentary majority, it cannot so easily ride down opposition from business or trade union groups outside the Commons. Insofar as laws need compliance by everyone, the case is strengthened for legislating by Consensus, since it is far easier to enforce legislation if it is not opposed by major interest groups in society. To avoid conflict in the implementation of legislation, a government with a secure parliamentary majority may adopt a "round table" approach, seeking agreement outside the House of Commons before introducing bills there.

Insofar as both parties perceive that the great bulk of the electorate (especially floating voters) agree about measures, then opposition to popular legislation would harm the party opposing it. This is also true insofar as legislation reflects Consensus between the government of the day and affected pressure groups. If pressure groups have reached a carefully negotiated agreement about a bill, MPs who oppose it will be unpopular because they threaten these understandings. The pressure on the opposition to drop an Adversary stance is particularly significant when the government of the day has achieved an agreement with the Trades Union Congress or the Confederation of British Industry, notwithstanding their nominal alignment with the opposition party.[1]

The pages that follow test whether the Adversary model fits the legislative record of the House of Commons as well as its procedures, or whether legislation, like electoral competition, shows both parties tending to conform to the Consensus model. The attitudes of MPs are examined first, followed by an examination of their actions in entering—or avoiding—the division lobbies. The concluding section shows how successive Parliaments cumulatively strengthen Consensus in the nominal home of Adversary government.

What MPs Think

Privately as well as publicly, MPs of different parties are prone to disagree with each other. The media and the party faithful encourage this as much as parliamentary procedure. Backbench MPs (and all MPs in opposition) have even more incentive than frontbench MPs to emphasize the differences between parties. Unlike frontbench leadership, backbenchers need not be constrained by the responsibilities of office. Instead, they can respond to partisan pressures arising from the Adversary element in party politics.

Because of the strength of party discipline, ordinary divisions on bills in the House of Commons normally do not provide ideal evidence of what MPs think. Divisions register what MPs are instructed to do by party Whips, not necessarily what they would do of their own volition. Most MPs agree most of the time with their Whips' recommendation, for MPs seek their job to advocate partisan views, and Whips cannot readily instruct a majority of their party to vote against their wishes. But there are always some who privately disagree while publicly assenting to their party's line. In the 1970s this has been made most evident by a steady trickle of ex-Labour ministers announcing that they can no longer support the programme of the Labour Party.

There are two major sources of evidence of the personal attitudes of MPs. The occasional free vote in the House on a contentious conscience issue gives individual MPs the chance to vote as they wish (or as constituency pressures dictate), free from party dictates, for no whip is issued. Unfortunately for purposes of analysis, free votes are not frequent, and the best systematic evidence comes from votes taken in the 1960s on a host of issues concerning the permissive society—hanging, divorce law reform, Sunday entertainments, the 1967 Abortion Act and the legalization of homosexuality.[2]

Even though conscience votes in the House of Commons are meant to be free of party discipline, Conservative and Labour MPs line up in accord with the Adversary model of party politics when voting according to individual decisions. The average index of interparty difference is 52 percent, equivalent to at least three-quarters of the MPs in each party voting against the other. Labour MPs have been particularly ready to show cohesion in votes on conscience issues; the average index of Labour cohesion is 73 percent. By contrast, Conservative MPs have tended to disagree about conscience issues, showing a relatively low index of cohesion of 31 percent. The divisions between the parties on conscience issues appear to be stable through the years. In 1969, all but one Labour MP voted in favour of the abolition of capital punishment, whereas 68 percent of Conservative MPs favoured its retention. In a vote on capital punishment in July 1979, once again all but three Labour MPs favoured the abolition of capital punishment, and 71 percent of Conservatives favoured its use.

An alternative way to assess the private views of MPs is to ask them to reply to questions about issues and, like a normal opinion poll, to offer respondents anonymity. This was done by a pair of American academics, Allan Kornberg and Robert C. Frasure, with the 1966–70 Parliament.[3] Five of their ten questions concerned matters of foreign policy, and five domestic issues; all were in fields where *prima facie* differences could be expected along party lines, particularly such issues as Rhodesia, immigration, comprehensive schools and the reform of trade unions.

In this opinion poll of MPs, the average index of interparty difference was 42 percent, equivalent to two-thirds in each party expressing Adversary opinions. The extent of cohesion within the Conservative Party was higher on "normal" governmental issues (61 percent) than on conscience issues (31 percent). Conservative cohesion was also higher than cohesion among Labour MPs, which was 53 percent in this survey of MPs' private opinions.

The available evidence of MPs' personal opinions confirms the expectation that Conservative and Labour members of the House of Commons disagree with each other from conviction, and not simply because of the dictates of the Whips. On ten of the fifteen issues for which data is available, a majority of Conservative MPs clearly disagree with a majority of Labour MPs, as the Adversary model postulates.

In disagreeing so definitely with each other, MPs differ from the electorate. As tables 3.3 and 3.4 showed, Conservative and Labour voters tend to share a Consensus outlook on many issues. Their average level of interparty difference (albeit calculated on different issues) was 18 percent, much less than that shown by MPs in their votes on conscience issues or in registering opinions privately. Labour MPs differ from Labour voters in showing a much higher level of intraparty cohesion. Membership in the Commons is associated with greater likemindedness among Labour MPs than among those they represent. By contrast, Conservative MPs are slightly less cohesive than their voters; Conservative politicians in the Commons have a broader outlook than ordinary Conservative voters.

Even though British MPs tend to disagree about specific political issues, they do not see themselves engaged in confrontation between forces of good and evil. Their adherence to Adversary policies is consistent with a Consensus acceptance of the legitimacy of differences between themselves and their parliamentary opponents. The point is demonstrated by a unique comparative survey of British MPs and Italian deputies, conducted by Robert Putnam, who interviewed nearly a hundred members of each Parliament in the late 1960s.[4]

On the basis of replies to a battery of questions designed to reveal intolerance, distrust, suspicion of opposition motives and rigid thinking about political attitudes, Putnam classified British MPs and Italian deputies according to their degree of generalized partisan hostility. The majority of British MPs ranked at the bottom end of the scale of partisan hostility, whereas the largest proportion of Italian deputies were high on partisan hostility (see figure 5.1). British MPs differ about who should govern and how the government should handle specific issues, but they do not see a gulf between themselves and their adversaries, as have Christian Democratic and Communist deputies in Italy.

Figure 5.1   Contrasting Levels of Partisan Hostility, Britain and Italy

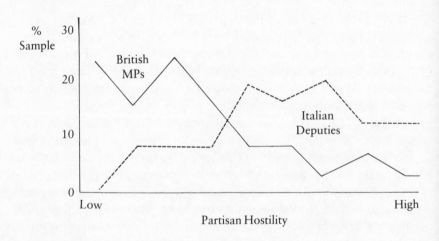

SOURCE: Adapted from Robert D. Putnam, *The Beliefs of Politicians* (New Haven: Yale University Press, 1973), figure 4.2.

What MPs Do

The bulk of the business of the House of Commons is determined by the initiatives of the government and not by opinion polls among MPs. As long as it has a majority in Parliament, the governing party can be virtually certain that any bill it introduces will be enacted into law. If the Cabinet has chosen wisely the grounds of the government's position, there will be little or no opposition within the majority party, and if the intended bill is popular and agreed to by pressure groups outside the House, the opposition may have difficulty in finding grounds to attack it.

The chief legislative question for the opposition party is *whether or not* to oppose a government bill. Because its decision will not affect the passage of legislation, the opposition party can take its decision on "purely" political grounds (i.e., in the light of its own tactical and strategic interests). Voting against a measure will not prevent it becoming law. For this reason, there is always an incentive for an opposition to vote against an unpopular measure, no matter how necessary it may be. The governing party does not enjoy this luxury.

The presence or absence of divisions on legislation give the clearest and most consistent evidence of which model of behaviour the parties in Parliament follow. To follow the Adversary model of party government, the opposition should normally vote against the legislation presented by the governing party. To follow the Consensus model, an opposition need not ask its MPs to vote with the government. It can give tacit consent to what is done by abstaining on a vote. At a minimum, this implies that it will not repeal the legislation subsequently.

In practice, the opposition party tends to follow the Consensus model in the House of Commons (see table 5.1). In second and third reading debates, aptly described as "the most important stage through which a bill has to pass, as its entire principle is at issue,"[5] the opposition divided the Commons against the government only 22 percent of the time from 1970 to 1979, the most politically contentious period in a generation.[6] The degree of Adversary voting was equally low in the 1970–74 Parliament (Labour voting against the government on 20 percent of bills) as in the 1974–79 Parliament (Conservatives dividing against the government on 23 percent of bills). *There were no significant divisions against the government on 78 percent of government bills.* Tacit consensus rather than outspoken opposition has been the rule.

Debates in the electorally partisan House of Commons are almost as uncontentious as debates in the nonelected House of Lords. In the

TABLE 5.1   *The Infrequency of Opposition Divisions against Government Legislation, 1970–79*

Session	No Division on Principle	Divisions on Principle (2nd or 3rd reading but less than 5 Committee divisions	Major Divisions (2nd or 3rd reading and 5 or more divisions, Committee stage
Labour			
Opposition			
1970–71	45	9	5
1971–72	35	4	6
1972–73	38	2	5
1973–74	23	4	1
	141 (80%)	19 (11%)	17 (9%)
Conservative			
Opposition			
1974	28	0	1
1974–75	30	7	15
1975–76	47	4	8
1976–77	25	11	2
1977–78	29	2	3
1978–79	32	3	0
Total	191 (77%)	27 (11%)	29 (12%)

SOURCES: I. Burton and G. Drewry, "Public Legislation: A Survey of the Session, 1974/75," *Parliamentary Affairs* 30, no. 2 (1977): 181, supplemented by their other annual reports published in *Parliamentary Affairs* 25, no. 2 (1972) et seq. Only divisions by official opposition included. Perennial and consolidation bills excluded.

1970–74 Parliament, there were divisions against the Conservative government on 22 percent of all public bills considered in the House of Lords, little different from divisions on 28 percent of legislation in the Commons.[7]

The tendency for Consensus to prevail is influenced by the issue at hand. The extreme of Consensus is registered on matters of national interest commonly affecting the whole electorate. Foreign affairs and defence are prototype examples of such issues. Issues central to the interests of one or both parties are less likely to be consensual. For example, legislation about trade unions is sensitive because the Labour Party is a federation of trade unions as well as individual members. Insofar as parties are expected to represent different socioeconomic interests in the electorate, then divisions should be frequent on economic and social policies that directly touch these interests.

The degree of parliamentary Consensus does vary with the type of issue (see table 5.2). There was only one divisive bill in international affairs (96 percent consensus) in the 1970s, and divisions on 31 percent of economic legislation. On social affairs, an area of major potential difference between the parties, the proportion of consensual bills was virtually average, 77 percent. Notwithstanding the alleged "incongruity" between party representation in Labour-dominated Scotland and Wales and an Anglocentric Conservative Party, there were fewer divisions than average on legislation for Scotland and Wales. The difference in frequency of divisions according to the issue should not obscure the main substantive point: There is normally Consensus on *all* subjects for legislation. Even in the contentious field of the economy, there were no divisions on two-thirds of all government bills.

One reason why divisions are limited is that a large proportion of government legislation is not about policy; instead it is concerned with the administration of government. After an intensive analysis of

TABLE 5.2   *The Subject Matter of Consensus and Adversary Bills, 1970–79*

| | Labour Opposition 1970–74 | | | | Conservative Opposition 1974–79 | | | |
| | Consensus | | Adversary | | Consensus | | Adversary | |
	N	%	N	%	N	%	N	%
Foreign and Defence	11	92	1	8	11	100	0	0
Home Affairs	31	89	4	11	45	92	4	8
Scotland and Wales	16	89	2	11	22	73	8	27
Social Policies	45	75	15	25	56	79	15	15
Economic Affairs	38	73	14	27	57	66	29	33
Totals	141	(80%)	36	(20%)	191	(77%)	56	(23%)

NOTE: Each measure is classified according to the minister introducing it. *Economic Affairs* includes Agriculture, Employment, Trade and Industry as well as the Treasury. *Home Affairs:* Home Office, Legal and Parliamentary measures. *Social Affairs:* Health and Social Security, Education and Environment.

Tabulations are for all government bills except perennial and consolidated legislation reaching 2nd reading in the Commons. Consensus bills are those without a division by official opposition at 2nd or 3rd reading; Adversary bills have such a division.

SOURCE: Derived from reports cited in table 5.1.

parliamentary legislation, Burton and Drewry distinguish two types of bills. *Policy* bills involve "substantial changes in public policy upon which there had already been public debate," such as the European Assembly Elections bill or the Scotland bill, as well as financial bills. By contrast, *administration* bills are measures that "sanction administrative changes, including changes in financial powers, to implement existing public policies."[8] Examples from 1977/78 are the Parliamentary Pensions bill and the Theft bill, amending a previous act that had not worked satisfactorily. (The authors admit that the distinction between policy and administration is difficult to apply in some instances). The distinction does *not* rest upon the amount of controversy a bill is expected to engender. A bill for a Cooperative Development Agency concerns policy but was not controversial, whereas the Iron & Steel Bill of 1977/78 affected administrative borrowing limits only but was controversial. Overall, the categories provide a reasonably reliable way of distinguishing between legislation that would be expected to be Adversary (i.e., policy bills) and that which should show Consensus (i.e., administration bills).

TABLE 5.3   *Divisions on Policy and Administration Bills, 1970–79*

	Labour Opposition 1970–74		Conservative Opposition 1974–79	
	N	%	N	%
Policy Bills				
No division on principle	67	69	92	67
Division on principle	14	14	16	12
Major divisions	16	17	29	21
	97	100%	137	100%
Administration Bills				
No division on principle	74	93	99	90
Division on principle	5	6	11	10
Major divisions	1	1	0	0
	80	100%	110	100%

SOURCES: Types of divisions defined in table 5.1. For a discussion of the categories of policy and administration, see Ivor Burton and Gavin Drewry, "Public Legislation: A Survey of the Session 1968/69," *Parliamentary Affairs* 23, no. 2 (1970): 161 ff.

The opposition is readier to oppose the governing party on policy issues than on administrative measures (see table 5.3). From 1970 to 1979 only one administration bill was the subject of a major division, and 8 percent subject to other divisions on principle. By comparison, one-third of all policy bills were the subject of divisions, including 19 percent that were the subject of a series of major divisions in the Commons. The reason for divisions occurring more frequently on policy bills is easy to understand. A measure that introduces a substantial change in public policy ought to be more important to the parties than a bill that simply alters means to established ends. Insofar as parties are Adversaries, there should be major divisions on policy bills. But since this occurred with less than one in five policy bills in the relatively contentious Parliaments of the 1970s, the Consensus model fits the policy initiatives of government as well as its administrative concerns.

A large measure of consensus between the front benches of the two major parties might be expected to cause dissent within the opposition party. Seeing their own leaders refusing to divide the House against the government, opposition MPs might consider this a "conspiracy of silence," unacceptable ideologically as well as tactically bad. Given opposition status, backbench MPs do not risk their party's losing office by moving a vote against their adversary. Moreover, dissent exerts pressure upon the opposition leadership to enunciate more distinctive policies, as a step to changes in public policy when the opposition next takes command of government.

In practice, the government of the day faces much more dissent from within its own ranks than from opposition MPs. A detailed analysis by Philip Norton of hundreds of dissenting votes in the House of Commons since 1945 shows that in 81 percent of all cases of backbench dissent, MPs in the governing party vote against their own leadership. Opposition MPs vote against their own leadership 39 percent of all dissenting divisions (see table 5.4). Only in the 1951–55 Parliaments, when the Labour opposition was unusually divided by the Bevanite controversy, did opposition MPs dissent more often than government MPs.

Dissent in government is not confined to Labour rule. The highest level of dissenting votes from government backbenchers was in the 1970 Parliament, when Conservative MPs dissatisfied with Edward Heath's measures produced 92 percent of all dissenting votes.[9] The proportion of dissenting votes accounted for by Labour MPs dissatisfied with the subsequent Wilson-Callaghan government fell in relative terms only because of continued dissenting votes by Conservative MPs in opposition. The extent of dissenting voting by government backbenchers rose in absolute terms by half from the 1970 to the 1974 Parliaments.

TABLE 5.4 *Backbench Dissent, 1945–79*

Parliament	% All Dissenting Votes Involving MPs Governing Party	% All Dissenting Votes Involving Opposition MPs	Dissenting Divisions N	% All Divisions
1945–50	91 Lab.	31 Cons.	87	7
1950–51	(100) Lab.	(33) Cons.	6	2
1951–55	44 Cons.	68 Lab.	25	3
1955–59	63 Cons.	53 Lab.	19	2
1959–64	88 Cons.	19 Lab.	137	13
1964–66	(100) Lab.	(100) Cons.	2	0.5
1966–70	88 Lab.	33 Cons.	124	9
1970–74	92 Cons.	15 Lab.	221	20
1974–79	71 Lab.	58 Cons.	448	28
Total	81% Government	39% Opposition	1069	

NOTE: Dissenting votes are those in which MPs divide against their own Whips or the clearly expressed view of their front bench.

( ) indicates unreliably small number of dissenting divisions for generalization.

SOURCE: Derived from Philip Norton, *Dissension in the House of Commons* (London: Macmillan, 1975), p. 609; and Philip Norton, "The Changing Face of the House of Commons in the 1970s," *Legislative Studies Quarterly* (forthcoming), table 3. Occasionally backbenchers on both sides of the House divide together; hence totals for two-party dissent exceed 100%.

The extent of dissent within a Parliament is limited. Until 1970 it rarely involved as many as one-tenth of all divisions, and only one-quarter since. Moreover, many instances of dissent involve only a handful of MPs in the governing party. In other words, the evidence of dissent does not detract from the overall pattern of Consensus voting in the Commons. What it does do is emphasize the low level of Adversary voting by the opposition.

The Adversary procedures of Parliament guarantee the opposition many opportunities on supply days to debate with the government on motions of the opposition's choosing. It can thus choose, several dozen times a year, the way in which to express its differences with the governing party, and if it wishes, to register this difference by its votes. The expectation is that the opposition will use its Supply Day motions to express critical differences with government. The more outspoken the attack that the opposition makes, the more it conforms to the Adversary model. If the opposition does not voice criticism or divide against the government on its own Supply Day motions, this supports the Consensus model.

When choosing its motion, the opposition can give full vent to an Adversary outlook by an outspoken attack on a specific policy, and dividing the House on it. A typical example of an Adversary motion is the following 1973 motion from the Labour opposition.

> This House condemns Her Majesty's Government for the bungled, inflationary and inequitable manner in which it has dealt with a mortgage rate crisis which is entirely due to the catastrophic failure of the Government's own housing and monetary policies.[10]

Alternatively, the opposition may wish to show that it not only dislikes what the government is doing but also has a reasoned alternative to put in its place. The reasoned alternative will not be worked out with the care of a government White Paper, but at least it purports to present the opposition as a party with an alternative policy, as well as objections to what the government is currently doing. A typical example is the 1976 Conservative opposition motion:

> That this House calls upon Her Majesty's Government to give positive encouragement to local authorities to sell council houses to tenants and to withdraw their ban on the sale of New Town houses.[11]

The opposition may wish to focus attention on the shortcomings of a particular departmental or ministerial policy without identifying its faults or proposing an alternative. It can do this by moving a token reduction in the estimates or in the salary of the minister. An even milder form of criticism is implied by the opposition simply initiating a wide-ranging discussion on an agreed topic by moving the emptiest of phrases: That this House do now adjourn.

The Conservative and Labour parties have differed in their style of opposition in the 1970s. The 1970–74 Labour opposition concentrated on outspoken attacks. More than three-quarters of its Supply Day motions were critical of particular policies, often in electioneering language, and Labour almost always divided the House at the conclusion of a debate to emphasize its Adversary sentiments. Only on a small number of occasions was it at a loss for something to criticize or internally divided about whether to criticize the work of the government, simply moving an adjournment amendment. Overall, the Labour opposition divided against the government at the end of 89 percent of its Supply Day debates (see table 5.5).

TABLE 5.5 *The Opposition Use of Supply Day Motions, 1970–79*

	Labour Opposition 1970–74			Conservative Opposition 1974–79		
	Divisions	Motions	Divisions as % all motions	Divisions	Motions	Divisions as % all motions
	N	N		N	N	
Outspoken attack	54	57	73	13	15	12
Reasoned	6	8	8	7	7	7
Reduction in salary	1	1	1	11	11	10
Adjournment	5	8	7	26	72	25
Totals	66	74	89%	57	105	54%

SOURCE: Compiled from *Hansard, Annual Index*, motions listed under Supply Days 1970–77; *Volume Index*, 1977–79.

By contrast, the Conservative Party has tended to be softspoken in opposition, dividing the Commons at the end of Supply Day debates little more than half the time (table 5.5). Conservatives have preferred to raise an issue by moving an adjournment motion rather than commit the party to a specific line of criticism of the Labour government. Moreover, the party did not divide the Commons at the end of nearly two-thirds of its 1974–79 adjournment motions. The Conservatives' unwillingness to engage in ceaseless divisions undoubtedly owed something[12] to the unusual parliamentary circumstances of a Labour government that lacked a secure parliamentary majority yet for nearly all its life was able to defeat votes of censure. Notwithstanding Mrs. Thatcher's wish to distinguish her party from the Labour government, the Conservatives did not wish to do this by repeatedly emphasizing their inability to defeat the government on critical motions in the Commons.

In the course of a year, MPs spend much of their time talking like Adversaries. But when the crunch comes, and the opposition is given the opportunity to vote against what the government of the day is doing, more often than not the opposition refuses to do so. Instead of incessantly dividing the House, the opposition tacitly accepts the enactment of legislation.[13] Even when forced by Supply Day procedures of Parliament to criticize the government of the day, an opposition does not necessarily press party differences to the point of voting against government policy. It is rare for an opposition to give overt consent to government policy by actually voting with it. This is not necessary; avoiding moving a division is enough.

From Tacit Consent to Moving Consensus

The durability of Adversary or Consensus legislation can be fully tested only when one Parliament succeeds another, and control of government changes hands. The party newly installed in office has the power to repeal all the laws that it had opposed in the previous Parliament.[14] Insofar as it does not do so, then previously Adversary acts become incorporated in the moving Consensus of government.

In practice, a government rarely moves the outright repeal of a bill enacted by its predecessor, no matter how hotly it is contested at the time. The reasons for this are several. Any bill, no matter how contentious, is likely to include measures considered to be desirable across party lines. Opposition is often voiced against one portion of a government's proposal and not its totality. A measure, even if as contentious as was local government reform in the early 1970s, can become proof against repeal if it has been implemented and "unscrambling" the Act would create great difficulties, as well as meet opposition from those now benefiting from the Act. A controversial bill may consolidate a number of previous acts; to repeal it outright would leave a void on the statute book. The point was well demonstrated when the 1974 Labour government came to repeal the Conservative government's contentious Industrial Relations Act of 1971. The first two clauses of the Labour government's Trade Union and Labour Relations Act 1974 declare:

1 The Industrial Relations Act 1971 is hereby repealed.

2 Nevertheless...(and the new Act catalogues a large number of clauses of the repealed Act that are then reenacted).

A newly installed government repeals little of the legislation enacted by its predecessor. When the Conservatives entered office in 1970, they used their powers of office to reverse only three measures that had been passed in the two previous sessions of Parliament: an annually renewable scheme for import deposits was allowed to lapse; a limitation upon rent increases in local authority housing was repealed; and Scottish local authorities were allowed to continue to pay fees for secondary education. In two of these cases, the Conservative government did not positively direct local authorities to reverse their policies; legislation simply allowed them to act differently. The Heath government did not alter dozens and dozens of measures that it had voted against in the previous Labour-controlled Parliament.

The return of a Labour government in 1974, following a Parliament in which Labour had opposed more than one-quarter of the Conservatives' bills, did not lead to a bonfire of Acts of Parliament. Labour did reverse eleven laws adopted by the previous Conservative Parliament. In particular, it repealed the 1971 Industrial Relations Act, a major Housing Finance Act, and a Conservative pension scheme. It also used its administrative powers to nullify Conservative legislation allowing museums and galleries to charge admission, and in place of the Industrial Reorganization Corporation, dissolved by the Conservatives, it created a National Enterprise Board. Important as these actions were, they affected only a handful of the total measures passed by the 1970–74 Parliament. Moreover, the measures reversed were less than half the number that Labour had itself opposed in the House of Commons. Whereas the Labour government had opposed British entry to the Common Market, the creation of independent local radio, National Health Service reorganization, the reorganization of local government and the Immigration Act of 1971, it did not repeal these bills once it had power in its hands.

When a general election is called in the middle of a session of Parliament, there is another opportunity to test whether Consensus persists from one Parliament to the next. All pending government bills lapse with the dissolution of Parliament. If control of government then changes hands at the election, the newly elected Cabinet is not committed to the lapsed bills. The Adversary model implies that none of the bills that die with a Parliament will be resurrected by its successor government. By contrast, the Consensus model implies that changing the governing party should not affect the course of legislation; bills proffered by one party could be reintroduced by their opponents in the new Parliament.

Political events provide two tests of the readiness of a new government to take over the legislation of its predecessor. The calling of a general election in June 1970 meant that 23 of the Labour government's pending bills lapsed before enactment. The Conservative government of Edward Heath entered office nominally pledged to major changes in the country's way of life. In its first session of Parliament, it reintroduced 14 of the 23 bills that its Labour predecessor had left stranded, including 6 policy measures. When the Labour government returned to office in March 1974, following the collapse of the "confrontation" administration of Edward Heath, it was faced with 22 bills that had not been completed in the previous session of Parliament. The Labour government reintroduced 15 of these 22 measures, including 11 policy measures.[15]

The Consensus model is clearly supported by taking 1970 and 1974 together. A majority of the bills left by a government of one political colour were taken over by their opponents upon entering office.

Whether one looks at the behaviour of MPs during a single session of the Commons or from one Parliament to the next, the conclusion is the same: Consensus best describes the legislative process. The conclusion is striking because it goes against the very character of the House of Commons as an Adversary institution. It is doubly striking because it is drawn from evidence of the 1970s, a period in which the rhetoric of Conservative and Labour MPs emphasized Adversary relations between the parties.

The systematic examination of the *whole* of the legislative record of Parliament corrects the distortion introduced by the perspectives of partisan MPs. Distortion is introduced by the sham image of Parliament as a setting of gladiatorial battles between two antagonistic parties. The fact that nearly four-fifths of legislation is not the subject of divisions of principle suggests that a coalition or minority government could carry most of the legislative work of government, for the difficulties of obtaining cross-party agreement in Parliament are much exaggerated.

The emphasis upon Adversary controversy in the media, in the rhetoric of Parliament and in party conferences distracts attention from the actual work of government. The bulk of government activity is not concerned with dramatic measures that are (and should be) hotly disputed between the parties. Instead, the bulk of government activities are so uncontroversial that they are never debated in Parliament, and if they are, tend to concern the administration of established policies more than issues of principle. To see government in Adversary terms is to mistake for the whole a relatively small part of its action leading to occasional divisions in Parliament.

Upon entering office, the first thing a government must face up to is its responsibilities under a great mass of *preexisting* legislation. If the government is to make a mark by introducing some new laws or altering some Acts of Parliament, it can gain the parliamentary time and political space to do so only by taking for granted nearly all the statutes already on the books. There is not world enough and time for a party in government to amend or even appraise all the laws for which it is responsible. The totality of legislation that a government carries out is not simply the product of its own volition. Instead, it is a compact between itself and its predecessors. The contents of that contract are dictated first of all by the laws that it inherits. Acceptance of these laws makes them part of the Consensus — and the addition of Acts by the new government makes the Consensus moving.

A newly elected government can make some difference to the legislation of a Parliament it controls. It makes decisions about what bills should be introduced, and which bills left by its predecessor should be abandoned. To drop a bill (for example, a Labour nationalization proposal or a Conservative tax concession) is an act of policy, albeit one that avoids sustained parliamentary controversy. A government can make decisions about the timing of legislation. It can determine whether a given proposal will be enacted in a Parliament it controls, or leave the prospect of action to a Parliament dominated by its opponents. Even though there may be good reasons to adopt a bill, the governing party may prefer to wait so that its opponents introduce legislation that its own supporters dislike.

When the government begins to draft a particular piece of legislation, it subjects most measures to considerable scrutiny, and even censorship, in order to minimize the controversy likely to be engendered. Measures are not put up to the Future Legislation Committee of Cabinet until controversial elements have been discussed with the interests affected, and, if possible, they have been "squared." A draft bill will not receive the endorsement of Cabinet unless and until controversial points in the legislation have been hammered out and often smoothed over in Cabinet Committees, and many of the objections that can be raised in the Commons will arise from interdepartmental matters. If a major measure is controversial between the parties (e.g., council house rents or the nationalization of an industry), a government with a working majority in the Commons will nonetheless introduce it. But table 5.1 demonstrates that "set piece" Adversary battles between the parties are relatively infrequent in the legislative calendar. Even though interparty Consensus is not required for passage, it is nonetheless the empirical norm in the enactment of parliamentary legislation.

The Consensus model fits the legislative work of the House of Commons because the government normally exercises political restraint. It does not use its undoubted legislative majority to carry through many controversial bills. Nor would it necessarily be well advised to do so. There is always the prospect of an electoral reaction against a governing party that adopts a bill generally unpopular with public opinion. Moreover, a bill strongly opposed in the Commons is likely to be strongly opposed by pressure groups outside the Commons, and the noncooperation of pressure groups can sometimes make it difficult to carry out a measure, even after it has become an Act of Parliament. In 1970–74 for example, the Labour opposition could only talk and vote against the Conservative Industrial Relations Act, whereas the unions, by noncooperation with government, could and did make the Act inoperative.

Legislation is the most durable work of each session of Parliament, but it is only made durable by consensual politics. The government of the day denies itself much of the power nominally granted by its absolute majority in order to ensure that most measures it introduces will receive the tacit support of the opposition party, as well as the active support of its own backbenchers. The government uses its control of legislation to avoid a large number of parliamentary battles, which can be counterproductive electorally and even more awkward in dealings with pressure groups. Much of the legislation that the government chooses to introduce is anodyne; it is primarily concerned with administrative problems or issues remote from election campaigns and party manifestos. After studying exhaustively the 1970–74 Parliament, in which political temperatures were relatively high, Burton and Drewry conclude:

> The legislative process remains very much characterized by consensus rather than by conflict. It may be true that an increasing amount of time has been spent (in adversary measures) but in absolute terms it is still not very much.[16]

CHAPTER 6

Reorganizing Government:
Partisanship without Technocracy

Constitutions assume consensus. Even if parties are Adversaries regarding specific policies, they are expected to agree about the "rules of the game" regulating the resolution of their conflicts. The continuity of political institutions in Britain, notwithstanding recurring changes of party government, is evidence of agreement about fundamentals. If the Constitution were at issue at every election, as in Northern Ireland, the conventional alternation of parties in office could not work. The twentieth-century histories of France, Germany and Italy show how party politics can lead to political upheavals in the absence of a consensus between parties about fundamental rules of the game.

The technocratic approach to constitutional engineering assumes the existence of consensus as well as technique. It starts from the assumption that everybody wants "good government" (hence, the American nickname of "goo-goos") and agrees about what good government is. Technocrats, whether management scientists or mannered mandarins, further assume that they have the expertise to produce changes leading to agreed ends.

The Adversary approach to government reorganization is succinctly expressed in the epigram of the American political scientist E. E. Schattschneider: "*Organization is the mobilization of bias.*"[1] Changing the form of government is only meaningful if it affects powers of decision. Schattschneider argues that any significant change in the workings of the policy process will confer advantages upon some groups and disadvantages upon others, altering the established balance of power. When change is mooted, the Adversaries may be political parties (e.g., if electoral rules are at stake) or the Adversaries may be institutionalized beneficiaries from the status quo (e.g., local authorities, civil servants or ministers) versus officials and groups expected to benefit from change.

At any given point in time, proposals for change are presented with the purported goal of making government "better" in some respect. The period covered by this book was unusual because of a widespread belief that something was fundamentally wrong with how Britain was governed. The optimists believed that whatever was wrong could be put right by changing the institutions of government in ways both consensual and technocratic. In the 1960s and early 1970s changes were proposed or adopted at every level of government from parish councils to Parliament,[2] as Harold Wilson and Edward Heath each presented himself as a "modernizer" of British government.

The purpose of this chapter is to see whether the changes in the rules of the game were carried out in a consensual and technocratic manner, or were adopted by Adversary politics. In the absence of a written Constitution, it is not easy to identify precisely what constitutes a constitutional change. The first section concentrates attention on Acts of Parliament that have a persisting effect upon political representation and the territorial extent of Parliament's authority. Efforts to reorganize the centres of government, Whitehall and Westminster, are then considered. Typically, these are measures that can be taken by a government of the day without parliamentary legislation, but not necessarily with the agreement of all within Parliament.

Changing the Rules of the Game

The Technocratic Consensus view of government assumes that there are agreed means to agreed ends. It follows from this that when legislation to effect change is put to Parliament, it should be accepted without division in the Commons. By contrast, the Adversary approach assumes that any change will be motivated by self-interest and thus cause opposition. Since the Constitution affects all the participants in the political system, Adversaries can come from outside as well as within Parliament.

Election Law

Laws concerning the election of Members of Parliament are central to party politics. Individual MPs cannot be indifferent to laws that may affect their chance of reelection, and party organizations cannot be indifferent to proposals that affect their chance of winning control of government.

The Representation of the People Act, 1948, was the single most important piece of electoral legislation introduced in the postwar period. It marked the conclusion of more than a century of reform initiated in 1832. The Act established the rule of one person, one vote, and abolished votes for University seats and the business franchise, and a host of lesser changes were made. The Conservative opposition strongly attacked the government for introducing a rule of one vote per person on the ground that it contravened recommendations of an all-party Speakers Conference on Electoral Law. But the recommendations to preserve plural voting and University seats, both in the Conservative interest, had been adopted in 1944, when the Conservatives were in a majority in the Commons. By 1948, the Labour Party was the majority party, and recommended what was in *its* interest. Conservative leaders attacked the Labour government, arguing a variation of the Manifesto doctrine, namely, that proposals that Labour agreed to in the 1944 Coalition were binding upon the Labour government after the 1945 election as well. When the Labour government not unsurprisingly rejected this argument, the Conservatives refused to vote for the Act on second or third reading.[3]

The redistribution of parliamentary constituencies touches individual MPs at their most sensitive point, as well as affecting parties collectively. Boundary Commissions were established by a consensus act of the Coalition government in 1944 and minor boundary alterations were made by agreement before the 1945 general election. However, the first postwar test in 1948 found the parties dividing as Adversaries along predictable lines of self-interest in response to a Labour proposal to give extra seats to urban areas, where Labour was strongest. The 1954 redistribution by Boundary Commissioners was the subject of very considerable local complaints in England. There were also unsuccessful protests in the courts against specific decisions of the English Boundary Commission. Acrimonious debates also occurred in the House because there were fewer voters in disproportionately Conservative rural seats than in disproportionately Labour borough constituencies. When redistribution orders were placed before the Commons, the Labour opposition unsuccessfully divided the Commons sixteen times.[4]

Redistribution was the cause of another Adversary conflict between the parties in 1969. The Labour Home Secretary, James Callaghan, introduced a bill to absolve the Home Secretary from presenting to Parliament until after the proposed reform of local government boundaries recommendations of Boundary Commissioners that were generally believed against the Labour interest. The Conservatives opposed the measure in the Commons and the House of Lords voted it down on 21 July 1969. In November 1969 the Home Secretary formally presented the Boundary Commissioners' recommendations for redistribution and recommended that Labour MPs reject them. Given the government's Commons majority, this was done. The Labour government also secured parliamentary endorsement of two other changes in electoral law, both reckoned to its own party advantage: reducing the voting age to eighteen, and lengthening the hours of polling to ten P.M. Conservatives voted against the proposals.[5]

Two proposed changes in electoral law were defeated in the 1970s because of a lack of consensus. In 1975 the Labour government established a *Committee on Financial Aid to Political Parties*[6] under Lord Houghton (a former Labour MP). The government arranged that at least five of the members were Labour supporters, and only one a recognized Conservative; the Labour Party's evidence strongly recommended public financial subsidies to parties. Notwithstanding this, the Houghton Committee could not itself find a consensus: seven members favoured state subsidies, one entered a reservation, and four members recommended against subsidies. No subsidy legislation was subsequently proposed because Labour was too weak in the Commons to enact financial subsidies to its advantage without a firm parliamentary majority.

The revival of interest in proportional representation since 1974 has ranged the Conservative and Labour parties against the Liberals on grounds of party interest, for proportional representation would very substantially increase the number of Liberal MPs and diminish the number of Labour and Conservative Members of Parliament. When the interests of the two major parties are not at stake, as in Northern Ireland, both parties have agreed to mandate proportional representation on Ulster for elections to its Assembly and to the European Parliament. But where their interests are immediately at stake in "mainland" Britain, the two parties have combined to defeat proportional representation for elections to the proposed Scottish Assembly and for elections to the European Parliament.

After a review of the politics of electoral reform since 1918, David Butler concludes with the hard but fair judgment:

> The electoral system, both in its broad working and in its detailed rules, is too important politically for party leaders to devolve decisions about it to others. The government, either unilaterally or after consultation with other parties, is going to use its parliamentary authority to get its own way.[7]

Ending Empire

In 1945, Westminster was responsible for the government of hundreds of millions of people in colonies scattered throughout the globe. By 1979, virtually all substance of that Empire had disappeared. In retrospect, the process of decolonization and independence appears inevitable. But at the time, the choices were neither consensual nor were they technocratic.

In virtually every colony, the Adversaries were indigenous independence parties against British government at Westminster. Initially the controversy was about whether a colony could achieve independence; the nationalist claim for self-government opposed the Imperial and Technocratic doctrine of "good" government. Then it became a controversy about the terms of independence, particularly where there were white settlers or other interests that Westminster wished to protect. The final disputes concerned the timing of independence; independence parties wished freedom *now,* without waiting for the evolution often envisioned in Colonial Office documents.

Disputes about decolonization started immediately after the war; the immediate issues were Indian independence and Britain's mandate in Palestine. They continued through disputes about the handling of the Mau Mau emergency in Kenya and the suspension of the Constitution of British Guyana in 1953; proposals to create a Central African Federation; withdrawal by Treaty with Egypt from the Suez Canal in 1954, and reentry by force in 1956; Cyprus; the secession of Rhodesia; and the Nigerian civil war. The controversies arose because of evidence that things were going wrong—or at least, "not all was well"—in whatever colony flashed into the news at the moment.

Controversies about decolonization did not follow the same course as controversies about domestic politics. Criticisms of the government frontbench by the opposition frontbench tended to be muted, in recognition of a common "national interest" and of limits upon the effective powers of Westminster. There was often a continuity of policy from government to government. Conservative governments found the "winds of change" accelerating the pace of decolonization against the wishes of many of their supporters, and Labour governments found it hard to secure their objectives (e.g., in Southern Rhodesia) when Parliament lacked *de facto* power. The frontbench tendency to agreement did not make Consensus prevail throughout Parliament. The Adversary attack on the government of the day, whatever its party, came from the backbenches, including Conservatives disturbed about the apparent speed of change and the Labour left concerned about methods used to maintain colonial authority and the alleged slowness of change.

The greatest Adversary controversies in decolonization arose within the colonies. Ultimately, any Consensus at Westminster was of little avail when Adversaries within a colony disagreed fundamentally about the post-independence government. Divisions within India eventually led to the creation of separate Indian and Pakistani governments, subsequently augmented by Bangladesh. The Palestine mandate was settled by force of arms between a newly proclaimed state of Israel and Arab states. Three major Westminster-engineered Constitutions — the Central African Federation, the East African Federation and the West Indian Federation — all failed to work because of internal divisions. Constitutional upheavals in many ex-colonies recurringly demonstrate that many nations of new construction lack political consensus. The upheavals also show that constitutions exported from Westminster have also failed the test of technocracy, lacking effectiveness as well.

The United Kingdom

Northern Ireland is a standing example of the limits of Consensus or Technocratic government within the United Kingdom. Within Northern Ireland, pro-British Unionist and Loyalist parties face an Adversary pledged to end the state of Northern Ireland, and make it part of a thirty-two-county United Ireland. Divisions on the Constitutional issue there have prevented anything resembling the alternation of parties in office, as at Westminster. From 1921 to 1972 Westminster backed a Stormont government that maintained one-party government there. Since 1972, Westminster has refused to consider the use of Westminster-style methods of governance in Northern Ireland, on the ground that the Province lacks sufficient consensus to play by the rules of the Westminster game.[8]

At Westminster, all the Northern Ireland parties stand apart from — and sometimes stand against — the major British parties. With the imposition of direct rule in 1972, the Ulster Unionists broke off from the British Conservatives, and Dr. Ian Paisley's Democratic Unionists never had any wish to affiliate. The Unionists' independence of the Conservatives was shown in the 1974–79 Parliament. The Labour Party broke its former loose affiliation with the Northern Ireland Labour Party, and the chief minority party, the Social Democratic & Labour Party, had greater links with Dublin than London. Moreover, its then leader, Gerry Fitt, provided a decisive vote to bring down the Labour government in the Commons on 28 March 1979.

The two frontbenches nominally responsible for the governance of Northern Ireland are, in effect, one party to the conflict. They have normally registered a Consensus. This is the more striking given the great and abrupt shifts in government policy in Northern Ireland. Not once did the opposition divide against any of the seventeen major Acts about the Province enacted by Parliament from 1968 to 1979, and on only one—the 1973 Border Poll—did the opposition even offer a significant amendment. On a number of these measures, however, there have been votes against legislation by MPs from Northern Ireland.

Devolution to Scotland and Wales arose as a constitutional issue from Adversary party politics. Support for the Scottish National Party and Plaid Cymru in 1966–67 and a further upsurge in 1974 challenged the parliamentary strength of both the Labour and Conservative parties. Insofar as the upsurge of nationalism represented a challenge to the unity of the United Kingdom, one might have expected the two main British parties to reflect a Consensus view in defence of the Kingdom. Insofar as devolution was intended to be a technocratic "good government" reform—a perspective taken by the largely apolitical Royal Commission on the Constitution—here again consensus might be expected. (In fact, the Commission itself could not agree about the optimum method of reform, and its members split half-a-dozen ways in their final report.) Insofar as devolution was a problem of party politics, the two major British parties, each with different interests in Scotland and Wales, would respond as Adversaries.[9] Initially, both major parties appeared to endorse devolution in principle in their October 1974 election manifestos.

The legislative history of devolution in the 1974–79 Parliament was a prime example of Adversary politics. The Labour government's actions were shaped by an immediate calculus of parliamentary votes. When only its own party discipline was at stake, the Labour leadership was prepared to see its first Scotland and Wales bill frustrated by its own backbenchers revolting against a parliamentary guillotine in February 1977. However, when the Liberals made devolution part of their price for a pact to support the government, Labour again pushed the subject forward.

The Conservatives consistently challenged Labour's bills to establish Assemblies in Edinburgh and Cardiff. The Scotland Act 1978 was opposed by the Conservatives at second reading, and in eighty-seven additional votes in the course of its enactment. The Wales Act 1978 was similarly opposed at second reading, as well as in a further sixty-three divisions. Exceptionally, the adversaries of the Labour government also included some Labour backbenchers. While the government secured en-actment of devolution bills for Scotland and Wales, in a necessary but atypical concession to its Adversaries, it allowed both measures to be tested by referendums there. The Welsh referendum unambiguously re-jected devolution, and the Scottish referendum did not provide substan-tial endorsement. Upon their return to office in May 1979, the Conser-vatives repealed both of their predecessor's devolution Acts.

The *reorganization* of local government structures enacted at the end of the nineteenth century was first mooted in 1947. Royal Commis-sions on London (1960), England (1969), Scotland (1969), a Local Gov-ernment Commission for Wales (1963) and a Review Body on Northern Ireland (1970) recommended major structural changes in local govern-ment for each part of the United Kingdom. Coincidentally, the timing of these reports allowed both Labour and Conservative governments to draft responses, because of intervening elections and changes of power at Westminster.[10]

The language of local government reform was full of technocratic phrases about efficiency and responsibility. But the practice of reform was a textbook example of Adversary politics. The new system for England and Wales introduced by the Conservatives' 1972 Local Gov-ernment Act differed from the earlier Labour government proposals. The Conservative government claimed that it would better realize generally valued goals; the Labour opposition claimed that it reflected partisan interests in local government, a charge that Conservatives could also hurl back against Labour's proposals. In the event, the bill was one of the most hotly contested in the 1970–74 Parliament, being opposed by Labour at second and third readings. The Local Govern-ment (Scotland) Act of 1973 was similarly the subject of controversy, and there were fifteen divisions on it in the Commons. In Northern Ire-land, the Local Government Act 1972 was passed by Stormont without division in its final months—but only because by that time the Irish Catholic opposition parties had already withdrawn from the legislature in protest against the entire constitutional position of the Province.

Change and Resistance at the Centre

Even if Westminster cannot control the periphery of its responsibilities, it should have the technical capacity and the will to resolve institutional problems facing it in SW 1. In the past two decades, there have been re-curring demands for something to be done about Parliament, about the major institutions of Whitehall and about the people found there. In Parliament, political resistance has prevented proponents of change from securing their objectives. In Whitehall, the lack of technology has meant that changes have not brought the satisfactions sought.

Demands to *reform Parliament* were first articulated by backbench MPs and academics in the early 1960s. The case for change was justified in technocratic terms of making the machinery of government work better. In the words of a leading campaigner, Professor Bernard Crick, they were promoted *"for the sake of the effectiveness of government itself."*[11] Reforms were directed toward improving MPs' scrutiny of government administration, providing more information and debate about major issues of policy and enhancing the lawmaking process. On the face of it, these generalized objectives are technocratic "good government" goals about which there might be interparty consensus.

In the Parliament of 1966–70, the Labour government did accept changes in House of Commons procedure and practice, ranging from such institutional experiments as select committees to such individual benefits as more services for MPs. A decade later, reformers reviewed what had happened — or rather, what had not been accomplished by the changes introduced — and concluded:

> .... how puny they are in the extent to which they have failed to grip the essential problem. One thing stands out clearly with hindsight (although some of us predicted it), which is that the main weakness of the parliamentary reform movement is that it did not presuppose political change, without which its innovations have been weakened almost to the point of impotence.[12]

The fundamental political conflict is not between the Labour and Conservative parties. Instead, the conflict is between inveterate backbenchers, whether Conservative or Labour, and frontbenchers enjoying the powers of office. To have real effect, any changes would have to strengthen MPs out of office. By definition, the opposition party lacks the votes to compel the government of the day to reform Parliament. The influence of government ministers ensures that the majority party will not vote to enhance backbenchers' powers when their partisan opponents are perceived as the prime beneficiaries.

If House of Commons reform were simply caught up in Adversary conflict between the Conservative and Labour parties, the swing of the electoral pendulum would sooner or later give a majority to the reformers. In fact, the adversaries are not evenly matched. The proponents of reform are *permanently* condemned to being on the "outs" with government. Quondam supporters turn into opponents of reform once they enter government and enjoy all the advantages of dominating an unreformed House of Commons.

The party in office has the power to reorganize *central government departments* by adopting "good government" measures to increase managerial efficiency, or for partisan advantage, or both. Since 1957 major changes have occurred in the departments of British government. Twenty-one departments have been abolished, and twenty-one new departments created. Such historic departments as the War Office, the Admiralty, the Colonial Office and the Board of Works have disappeared from Whitehall, and new Departments such as Defence, Environment and Industry have emerged. Some, such as the Ministry of Technology and Land and Natural Resources, have been created and abolished within this period.

Changes in government departments do not appear to reflect a pattern of Adversary politics. The greatest number of changes, sixteen, was made under the 1964–70 Labour government; the second largest, ten, under the 1970–74 Conservative government, with nine under the Conservatives from 1957 to 1964, and seven in five years of Labour government from 1974. Changes are not so much a reflection of partisan differences as a response to the very widespread mood to reform many major British institutions in the decade from 1964 to 1974, and the personal interest of two Prime Ministers (Harold Wilson and Edward Heath) in the organization of government. When the government of the day required legislation to "hive off" the Post Office in 1969, the Property Services Agency in 1972 and employment services in 1974, all three bills went through without a major division in the Commons.

In organizations concerned with the economy, successive governments act as if confronted with a dilemma. First one alternative is tried and then another. In 1964, the Labour government entered office with the intention of stimulating economic growth. It established two novel ministries, the Department of Economic Affairs and the Ministry of Technology. The Department of Economic Affairs was abolished in October 1969, and the Ministry of Technology by the incoming Conservative government. The Conservatives responded to the same problem by creating a mammoth Department of Trade and Industry. In 1974, the incoming Wilson government split this into separate departments of

Trade and of Industry and, in response to inflation, created a Department of Prices and Consumer Protection. In 1979 Mrs. Thatcher abolished this last innovation, but retained Industry and Trade. Sir Richard Clarke, who was closely associated with thinking about organizational change in Whitehall, wrote the following epitaph on the attempt to find the "right" organizational form for the industrial problems facing government:

> There was no stable or satisfactory organizational situation. There was a continuous process of change, sometimes well conceived and sometimes less so; and it is difficult in retrospect to recognize any of these changes from which a clear national benefit can be said to have resulted.[13]

While efforts to reform central government departments have brought changes, many can best be described as "change without reform," for the evidence of improvement is difficult to discern. One reason for this is that there is little in the way of cause-and-effect understanding of what types of organizational forms are best suited to different policy problems. A second reason is that many problems are intrinsically dilemmas: The benefit in making one change tends to be matched by resulting difficulties. In such circumstances, changes involve trading in one problem for another.

The *personnel* of central government have also been subject to pressures for change that reflect a consensus among Conservatives and Labour politicians that "something" needed doing about the civil service. Alterations have occurred in the personnel of Whitehall since the 1960s, with Adversary differences between politicians and civil servants muted, and apparently now resolved. While the results have been for the most part consensual, they have lacked substantial evidence of technocratic effectiveness.

In the 1960s, the senior civil service became self-critical of its conventional practices at the same time as it was being criticized by noncivil servants as a major cause of "What's wrong with Britain." The Fulton Committee on the Civil Service was established in 1966 to make a full-scale review of the civil service. Its establishment was strongly supported by Sir Lawrence Helsby, the civil servant in charge of the civil service. The membership was appropriately consensual: Sir Edward Boyle and Shirley Williams were appointed as the Conservative and Labour MPs, and the senior civil service was also well represented.

The Fulton Committee's *Report* was generally critical of the civil service, asserting: "The structure and practices of the Service have not kept up with changing tasks. The defects we have found can nearly all be attributed to this."[14] Yet it was also careful to emphasize that its criticisms were part of a consensus.

> Reviewing the evidence as a whole, we have been struck by a remarkable consensus of opinion. Many tributes have been paid to the strong qualities of the Civil Service. At the same time, there is a large measure of agreement on the major problems that now need to be solved, and on some of the reforms that should be introduced for this purpose.[15]

When the Fulton Committee's recommendations were published, there was consensus endorsement in the House of Commons; they were welcomed by Edward Heath, as leader of the opposition, as well as by the Prime Minister.[16]

Subsequent actions to reform the civil service have been taken without political controversy. Change has been consensual because, as L. J. Sharpe notes, "These changes have been largely in the hands of those to be changed," that is, civil servants themselves.[17] But changes have not been technocratically effective, nor did the *Report* have an explicit, coherent and well-substantiated model of how the reforms proposed could achieve identified goals. This was illustrated by the Fulton Committee's recommendation that recruits to the senior civil service should have "relevant" knowledge of the work of government. It could not agree among itself about what subjects were particularly relevant to the work of government, or how relevance could best be assessed.[18] In consequence of willing an end without a means, the recommendation came to nothing.

Good Government: Intentions Are Not Enough

The foregoing review of reorganization in British government shows that the Adversary model often describes the political process in which major organizational changes in British government are mooted. Even if there is agreement upon goals in the abstract—and "good government" is a *very* abstract term indeed—there is normally disagreement about particulars. The simplest way to predict who will oppose change is to see whose ox is gored.

The Conservative and Labour parties have consistently been Adversaries on legislation to change election laws, to alter the distribution of powers between Westminster and Scotland and Wales, and to reorganize local government. The conflict can be explained by the fact that the parties have differing interests. For example, Conservatives have more elderly voters and Labour more younger ones; this determined which party proposed lowering the voting age. The 1964–70 Labour government's proposed reorganization of local government was regarded as inimical to the interests of Conservative councillors. The 1970–74 Conservative government therefore altered the plans for reorganization.

Where frontbench consensus does exist, it does not necessarily follow that the issues are without controversy. If this were the case, they would be "apolitical." In the case of decolonization, the chief Adversaries were nationalist groups demanding independence vs. government at Westminster. In Northern Ireland, the Adversaries dispute differences with bullets as well as ballots. In both cases, it could be argued that there is consensus within Westminster, albeit this is incapable of "depoliticizing" the issue. As far as the reform of Parliament itself is concerned, there is frontbench consensus that backbenchers should be kept weak; this does not end disagreement but only buries it because of the hegemony of the front benches in Parliament.

Two issues considered here—the reorganization of central government departments and the civil service—have been treated as Consensus matters by successive Labour and Conservative governments. The leaders of both parties agree about the desirability of getting the machinery of government "right," and recruiting and training the "best" people as civil servants.

The difficulty in reforming central government has not come from Adversary controversies, but from technocratic ignorance. Notwithstanding good intentions, neither politicians, management scientists nor conventional specialists in public administration have been able to predict the effects of reorganization. Technicians have secured Consensus about goals, but they have lacked technique. Reforms have been urged more as an act of faith than as the application of a known technology. Major changes have occurred in Whitehall because there was a consensus about the desirability of proposed actions—and not because there was a well-substantiated case showing how desired effects would be achieved by proposed changes. Well-intentioned persons recommending institutional change have a "good" government "impulse to solve problems, not understand them."[19]

Instead of speaking about British government as if it were a piece of machinery, if would be better to represent it by the metaphor of an athletic arena. Government can be the scene of Adversary competition between two teams. Those involved are serious about who wins, and how well each side plays. All accept the rules of the game, just as party politicians accept the Constitution. But having done that, all play to win. Government institutions can only change as part of a political process. When debates arise about major constitutional issues in British politics, parties agree about how to appraise a proposal, but not about the answer each gives to the simple question: What's in it for us?

CHAPTER 7

Managing the Economy:
Neither Technocracy nor Ideology

The government's resources for managing the economy are very different from its resources for enacting legislation or changing its organizational structure. Whereas government may claim to be sovereign over legislation, it cannot pretend to be sovereign over the economy. A law is expected to be obeyed, whereas a ministerial statement about full employment may be followed by a rise in unemployment. The constraints upon the government's economic policies are both national and international. In the mixed economy of Britain, both trade unions and business firms have powers independent of government and can influence — or ignore — government in many respects. International influences also affect the state of the economy, for better (the windfall of North Sea oil) or worse (rising imports and relatively declining exports).[1]

Conventionally, the Conservative and Labour parties have been assumed to pursue Adversary economic policies. The cause is said to be the intrinsic character of each party, and not the machinery for electoral or parliamentary competition. Because the Labour Party calls itself a Socialist party, it is expected to seek (and make) structural changes in the economy whenever it is in office. Conservative opponents display a fear of the Labour Party being Socialist, just as left-wing critics of the Labour leadership attack it for not being Socialist enough. Similarly, the Conservatives are reckoned to manage the economy or "serve" business interests — even though businessmen can sometimes complain bitterly about such consequences of Conservative policy as the inflation and embittered industrial relations occurring under the Heath administration.

Even if the philosophical or rhetorical commitments of the parties are dismissed as window-dressing, their profile of electoral support and party finance identifies the parties with economic interests. The Labour

Party is closely tied to the trade unions and the interests of manual workers, whereas the Conservatives are closely identified with the middle class and better paid groups in society, endorsing the use of the market to meet society's needs through the private, not the public sector.

If the economic interests and the ideologies of different groups in British society are in conflict, and the two parties represent these conflicting interests, the Adversary model ought to predict how an election outcome will affect the management of the economy. So certain are many people of a necessary change in direction of economic policy that a major critique of British economic performance in the 1970s starts from the assumption that the Adversary system causes economic instability as policies change abruptly with the alternation of Conservative and Labour governments.[2]

Yet it is equally plausible to assume a Consensus approach to the management of the economy. Many of the goals of economic policy are positively valued by all parties. There is no difference between Conservatives and Labour in their desire to keep unemployment and inflation down and to keep up the balance of payments and economic growth. Whatever the interests or ideology of the party in opposition, once in office a party may concentrate upon delivering the goals that are popular. And the electorate wishes the party in office to achieve all these goals.

In the era under review here, economics promised to provide politicians with the technocratic means to guide the economy to achieve Consensus goals. From the 1950s to the 1970s there was widespread political acceptance of the basic Keynesian demand management model of the economy. The Keynesian model was reckoned to be scientific, allowing policy makers to deduce from it the causal consequences of government adopting one policy rather than another. It was politically acceptable because it did not prescribe which particular objective—economic growth, full employment or the reduction of inflation—should receive the highest priority at any given time. Nor did it prescribe that politicians should always pursue the same goal. It left politicians with the power to vary policies according to circumstances.

The Technocratic model makes the Treasury, not the party system, the central institution for managing the economy. The Treasury is the premier department within Whitehall because of its necessary importance in managing the expenditure of other government departments, as well as managing the economy as a whole. Its power and prestige enable it to recruit many of the ablest persons entering the higher civil service, as well as recruiting British economists with good international reputations as advisors. Once Treasury recommendations are endorsed by the Chancellor of the Exchequer, he can use his political standing within the Cabinet to secure government endorsement.

A Whitehall perspective on the economy suggests that its management is best described by combining two models into a single model of policy making by *Technocratic Consensus*. Whatever the intentions of a party newly installed in government, its practice should agree with the actions of its predecessors, because technical considerations dictate what a government must do. The optimist might expect economic science to provide an optimal way to manage the economy. A pessimist might reckon that the constraints upon the British government are so great that there is only one policy that it could adopt at any given point in time. In either case, even though the party in government changes, technocratic policies remain constant.

The Technocratic Consensus model predicts similarities in practice in the economic policies of different parties, whereas the Adversary model predicts major differences. The purpose of this chapter is to test which, if either, of these models better fits the record of the British economy since 1957. Before this can be done, the model of Technocratic Consensus must itself be clarified, and this is done in the section that follows. The second section tests the resulting models against the inputs to the economy that government can control: interest rates, the public sector borrowing requirement and public expenditure. The third section tests the models against economic outcomes: economic growth, earnings, the distribution of income and wealth, employment and inflation. The concluding section discusses the model that best fits the record of two decades of government management of the economy in Britain.

Expanding the Alternatives

The Technocratic Consensus model does not require that government and opposition parties agree at a given moment; their contrasting political positions can allow them to respond differently on grounds of electoral tactics, interest-group pressures or ideology. From a citizen's point of view, how the parties behave when each is in power is more important than how either may act when out of office. The Technocratic Consensus model is concerned with how different parties act at different points in time when each is in the same position—government. It postulates that once an opposition party enters office, it will in practice follow the same policies as its predecessors because it is subject to the same incentives and constraints.

An economy, by definition, is about activity through time. Factors of supply and demand are constantly in flux. Daily events may produce seemingly small changes, but if these changes reverse trends, making unemployment or inflation rates go up or down, they excite great political attention. Even more important, small annual changes in the growth of the national product, of public expenditure, or both can cumulatively compound to make a big difference to the nation.[3]

The *fatal flaw* of the Technocratic Consensus model is that it implies an unreal constancy in public policy. In its simplest form, it posits:

> *Labour government practice* is equal to
> *Conservative government practice*

As long as comparisons are only made between successive pairs of governments, then the Technocratic Consensus model appears to be a simple extension of the Consensus model of the party system. But the Technocratic Consensus model is explicitly concerned with change — or rather, the *absence* of change — through many years. As one government succeeds another, the identity of economic policy extends further and further across time. By a simple process of substitution, it implies:

> *Labour government practice (1945–51)* is equal to
> *Conservative government practice (1970–74)*

> and

> *Conservative government practice (1957–64)* is equal to
> *Labour government practice (1974–79)*

> and even

> *Labour government practice (1964–70)* is equal to
> *Conservative government practice (1979—)*

In effect, the Technocratic Consensus model declares that the direction of the British economy should not vary in a period of twenty to thirty-five years, encompassing administrations that on the face of it appear as different as those of Clement Attlee, Harold Macmillan, Harold Wilson, Edward Heath and Margaret Thatcher.

The identities assumed by the Technocratic Consensus model are of decreasing plausibility, the longer the length of time that the chain of logic is stretched. Yet they are not *ipso facto* absurd. Just as the incoming government inherits all the Acts of Parliament of its predecessors, so too it inherits an economic system created by a very lengthy historical process. In the very short run it may only be capable of making changes at the margin. For example, to speak of "restructuring" an economy in the course of five years is to voice a pious aspiration, not a practical target.

The Adversary model is not so much concerned with the long-term course of the economy as it is with its immediate direction. In the course of five years a governing party can at least hope to reverse the direction of major economic trends, encouraging the rate of economic growth to go up and the rate of inflation and unemployment to go down. Since relatively small percentage changes can involve big sums—a 1 percent increase in growth adds upwards of £2 billion to the national product and a 1 percent increase in unemployment 250,000 to the dole queue—even seemingly small changes in direction can be of major political significance.

In effect, there are at least four alternative ways of viewing the management of the economy when control of government passes from one party to another.

1. Reversal by Adversaries

This model, like its counterpart for parliamentary legislation, starts from the assumption that the two major British parties have different outlooks. It differs from the parliamentary model, for it is concerned with policies through time. When different parties control government, they are expected to act differently. Insofar as party manifestos stress differences in economic policies, then this model is also consistent with the Manifesto model.

Given that every government has a multiplicity of economic objectives, some of which must be sacrificed or traded off in pursuit of others, it would be entirely plausible for a Labour government to pursue low unemployment and accept high inflation, and a Conservative government to do the opposite. These differences could persist indefinitely as parties alternate in office. A governing party "overshooting" one target might well bring the other party into office to reverse direction. Reasoning from *a priori* assumptions about presumed differences in party values, one might expect inflation to be generated by a Labour government's attempt to reduce unemployment, and be followed by a Conservative government that would reduce inflation, until the resulting rise in unemployment lost it an election and let Labour "cure the Conservative remedy" by another dose of reflation. In formal terms, the Reversal by Adversaries model can be stated as

Conservative government 1 is equal to *Conservative government 2*
is not equal to
Labour government 1 is equal to *Labour government 2*

2. Random Situations

The opposite of a completely static and predictable technocratic system is one in which changes are as frequent as situations require, but random. Most historians appear to subscribe to a random theory of governance. They expect each government to differ uniquely from its predecessors and successors, according to the situation, which is seen as a random distribution of personalities, events and external circumstances. In terms of the management of the political economy, a random situation model posits that there is no pattern in the relationship between the party in office and the performance of the economy. An oil crisis or an electoral misadventure might lead the governing party — any party — to deviate from Adversary or Technocratic norms.

A random situation model does not deny the possibility of identities between policies pursued by different governments. It simply states that there is an *equal probability* that a Conservative government will follow the same economic policies as a Labour government as there is that it will resemble a Conservative government, and vice versa. In formal terms:

Probability (Con govt 1 equals Con govt 2)
equals
Probability (Con govt 1 equals Labour govt 1)
equals
Probability (Labour govt 1 equals Labour govt 2)
equals
Probability (Labour govt 1 equals Con govt 2)
et sequentia

Two models of party management of the economy are variants of the Technocratic Consensus model. They accept the importance of technical determinants of economic policy, but they do not assume that conditions remain static.

3. The Dilemma Cycle

A dilemma, by definition, implies both stasis and movement. There is stasis insofar as the alternatives that constitute the dilemma are fixed. There is movement insofar as there is a choice to be made, and reasons for selecting each of the choices. A dynamic cycle results as government alternates policies between the horns of the dilemma. The pattern of change may take more than one form. A Labour government might enter a stop-go dilemma cycle by choosing less unemployment, until the resulting "overheating" of the economy so increases inflation that it switches to the other horn. A Conservative government might be expected to enter the cycle at the other end, deflating the economy to reduce inflation at the price of rising unemployment until the latter reaches a level considered unacceptable, and the stop-go cycle starts again. Another dilemma is the choice between doing what is electorally popular but economically harmful or what is economically desirable but electorally unpopular. In this dilemma, the cycle is determined by nearness or distance from an election.[4]

The Dilemma Cycle proposes that the major changes in economic policy take place *within* the lifetime of a party in office. Whatever policy a governing party initially adopts because of perceived benefits will increasingly become untenable because of its costs. In the course of a Parliament, a governing party will in turn try *all* the available policies at hand, without being fully satisfied by any. The variations in economic policy during the life of a government are likely to be similar notwithstanding differences in party labels.

Variation in Conservative govt 1
equals
Variation in Labour govt 1
equals
Variation in Conservative govt 2
equals
Variation in Labour govt 2

4. Secular Trend

Many public policies involve slow but steady changes in more or less the same direction for a period of years, as incremental changes do not oscillate as in a cycle but show a systematic trend in one direction. For example, while growth rates of the economy are not absolutely steady, they normally show an increase in the national product from one year to the next. Major economic policies may follow a secular trend, whether determined by the positive actions of government or, in the case of the contraction of an industry, by negative forces that government cannot stop. A secular trend need not be inevitable. As long as it continues for a number of years, notwithstanding the alternation of parties in office, it will reflect forces more powerful than the policies of Adversary politicians. If the trend is benign, it will also be preferable to constant change because of the electoral cycle.

The Secular Trend model posits that regardless of party, the more distant in time two governments are, the less likely they are to resemble each other. Formally, the Secular Trend model states:

> *Conservative govt 1*
> is less than
> *Labour govt 1*
> is less than
> *Conservative govt 2*
> is less than
> *Labour govt 2*

In the course of a Parliament, every government has ample opportunity to establish a pattern of economic policy. The patterns of successive Conservative and Labour governments can be compared with precision because the inputs of economic policy and economic outcomes are measurable in quantitative terms. Moreover, in the course of two decades, there are ample opportunities to observe whether there are trends, cycles or random fluctuations between and within periods of party government. The graphs on the following pages plot the annual performance of successive government economic policies from 1957 to 1979. The trend lines superimposed on the graphs show whether the party in office makes a difference to economic policy or is simply riding a dilemma cycle or a trend.*

* The *correlation* statistic indicates the degree of association between time and the economic condition that is the subject of the graph; the r^2 *statistic*, the proportion of the total variation explained by time; and the *B value*, the average annual change in the economic condition measured on the vertical axis of the graph.

The *significance* figure shows the number of times in 100 that the association cited is likely to result from chance; by convention, anything below .05 is considered statistically significant, and a significance level of .01 or less is extremely unlikely to reflect chance relationships.

Where official data sources permit, calculations are made for "adjusted calendar years," that is, indicators cited for election years divided at a point near polling day to produce "years" of unequal length as follows: January–October 1964, October 1964–December 1965, January–June 1970, June 1970–December 1971, January 1973–March 1974, March–December 1974, January 1978–May 1979.

Because every British government faces a multiplicity of economic problems, it must make a series of choices about relative priorities (should economic growth or price stability come first?); about the means to be used to secure its chief priorities (pump-priming public deficits or strict control of the money supply?) and about whether to hold firm to initial priorities as their costs become evident and events threaten to force the government off its original course. In such circumstances, a governing party has many chances to reveal distinctive priorities, whether different from its opponents or different from its own previous manifesto statements. It does not make once-for-all decisions about economic policy; instead it must constantly consider altering particular policy inputs if they fail to produce desired economic outcomes, "fine" or "rough" tuning economic policies intended to produce desired outcomes.

Government Inputs

Immediately, the most important set of economic indicators are those that measure a government's *inputs* to the economy. A government can claim "diminished responsibility" for many economic outcomes, explaining them away as the result of national or international forces beyond its control. But it cannot claim that it lacks influence on such important inputs to the economy as interest rates, the extent of public borrowing or total public expenditure. In practice, both Conservative and Labour governments regard these three economic policies as major influences on the national economy.

At any given point in time, the government of the day can follow one of three alternative policies on *minimum lending rate* (formerly, bank rate); it can raise it, lower it or let it stand as it is. In Keynesian economic theory, no government is expected to keep the minimum lending rate constant at 2 percent, as was the case from 1932 to 1939, or from 1940 to 1951. Since then the bank rate has been expected to move in accord with the government's economic intentions, rising to reduce inflationary pressures and falling when government wishes to stimulate the economy. On *a priori* grounds, the Dilemma Cycle is the model best suited to the anticipated ups and downs in the minimum lending rate.

Instead of the minimum lending rate rising and falling between relatively fixed positions from 1957 to 1979, there has been a constant tendency for the rate to rise higher and higher regardless of the party in office. Under the 1957–64 Conservative government, bank rate averaged 5.1 percent with a maximum of 7 percent. Under the 1964–70 Labour gov-

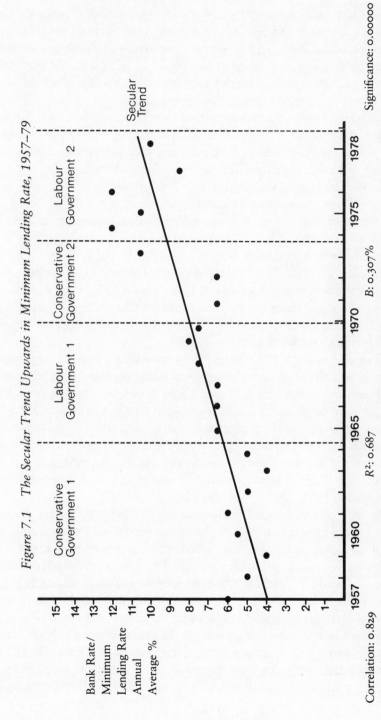

Figure 7.1 The Secular Trend Upwards in Minimum Lending Rate, 1957–79

Correlation: 0.829   R²: 0.687   B: 0.307%   Significance: 0.00000

SOURCE: Adjusted averages calculated from *Economic Trends* (London: HMSO) Annual supplement, 1979, p. 174; and H. M. Treasury *Financial Statistics* (London: HMSO), July 1979, table 13.11. Prior to 1972 Minimum Lending Rate was known as Bank Rate.

ernment it averaged 7.0 percent with a maximum of 8 percent. The 1970–74 Conservative administration pushed the lending rate as high as 13 percent, and it averaged 7.4 percent. The 1974–79 Labour government pushed the lending rate up to 15 percent in 1976, and it averaged 10.5 percent. Within a few months of entering office, the Thatcher government went even further, raising the minimum lending rate to 17 percent. While there are fluctuations in minimum lending rate when each party is in office, the changes do not reflect a movement back and forth between fixed points, as in a dilemma cycle. Instead, successive governments, regardless of party, have tended to increase lending rates.

Notwithstanding the alternation of nominally "dear money" Conservative administrations and nominally "cheap money" Labour governments, there has been a secular trend upwards in the minimum lending rate for two decades. The data displayed in figure 7.1 reject the idea that party government in Britain means a reversal of policy as adversaries change place in office. Nor is there any sign of randomness in the movement of the average lending rate from year to year. There is a significant and strong correlation between the minimum lending rate and the passage of time. Secular forces can explain 68.7 percent of the change in the minimum lending rate from 1957 to 1979.

The *public sector borrowing requirement* is a second important means by which the government of the day can regulate its expenditure and thus influence the economy as a whole. A budget surplus is normally thought to be desirable by conservative (and Conservative) standards of fiscal management, and a budget deficit acceptable (or even desirable) by Keynesian doctrines of demand management and Labour advocates of the increasing socialization of the economy. Partisan economic doctrines thus suggest that the pattern of public sector annual deficits and surpluses would fit the Adversary model of governing.

In fact, public sector borrowing does not differ by party; deficits were incurred in twenty of the years from 1959 to 1979.[5] Deficits occurred in eight of the ten years of Labour government and in every year of Conservative government. Whether Conservative or Labour, the government of the day tends to practice one-eyed Keynesianism; it responds positively to demands for a deficit to stimulate the economy, but not to signs that a budget surplus should be adopted to deflate it.[6]

Public sector borrowing through the years shows a secular trend upwards, and a dilemma cycle around the trend in the 1970s. When the effects of inflation are discounted by measuring deficits in terms of constant value pounds, the deficit has been increasing on average by £400

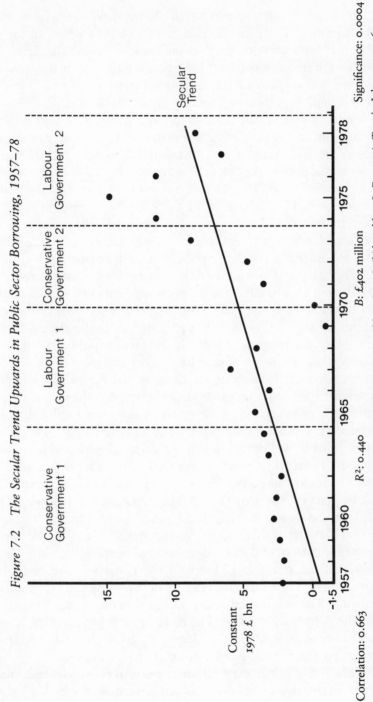

Figure 7.2   The Secular Trend Upwards in Public Sector Borrowing, 1957–78

Correlation: 0.663   R²: 0.440   B: £402 million   Significance: 0.0004

SOURCE: Calendar year data from *Economic Trends* (Annual Supplement 1976), table 116; 1978, ibid., table 138, *Economic Trends*, July 1979, p. 56.

million annually (figure 7.2). Overall, the trend explains 44 percent of the total variance. There are fluctuations around the trend. In the period from 1957 through 1966, the fluctuations were very slight. The 1964–70 Labour government was "off line" because the deficit was well below average, and surpluses were actually achieved in 1969 and 1970. From then through 1975 there was a steady upwards trend in the deficit. Since that time, public sector borrowing has fluctuated up and down. The fluctuations in the public sector borrowing requirement in the 1970s reflects the dilemma of a government trying to fight unemployment by an increased deficit, yet also anxious to avoid so large an increase that it stimulates inflation. The fluctuations in the budget, like the trend, are not determined by changes in the party in office. Primarily, they reflect powerful economic forces that have increased deficits under both Labour and Conservative governments and concurrently increased pressures to undertake restrictive policies to curb borrowing.

Public expenditure is doubly important, for it is the means by which government tries to influence the economy generally, as well as making specific decisions about which programmes it wishes to favour or curtail. Labour favours the Welfare State programmes that collectively account for the largest part of the budget. It also favours public expenditure for its own sake, as a means of socializing more and more of the nation's economic product. By contrast, the Conservative Party dislikes high levels of public expenditure on principle, believing that the nation's wealth is better off in private hands. Conservatives also favour reducing the taxes necessary to finance public expenditure and encouraging the use of privately financed welfare services in education, health and pensions. On grounds of party doctrine, whether the Conservative or Labour Party is in office should make a big difference to patterns of public expenditure.

In practice, the growth of public expenditure has shown a steady secular trend upwards through the years, varying little with the complexion of the party in office (see figure 7.3). Once in office, parties do not reverse the pattern of their predecessor; public spending has increased in constant price terms in eighteen of the twenty-one years from 1957 through 1978. The Conservatives have not even enjoyed the "luxury" of a recurring dilemma, for public expenditure has risen in real terms in every year the party was in office. The three times it has declined have been under Labour governments, which went against the grain of party doctrine as part of a package of anti-inflationary policies.

The rise of public expenditure appears to be largely determined by inertia forces outside the control of any government, whether Labour or

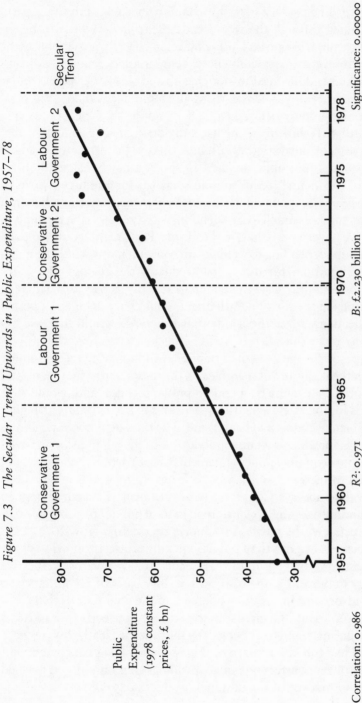

Figure 7.3 The Secular Trend Upwards in Public Expenditure, 1957–78

Correlation: 0.986

R²: 0.971

B: £2.230 billion

Significance: 0.00000

SOURCE: For 1957–68, Central Statistical Office, *National Income and Expenditure* (London: HMSO, 1968), table 53; for 1969–70, ibid., 1973, table 51; for 1971–75, ibid., 1975, table 10.2; for 1976–77, ibid., 1977, table 9.4; 1978 estimated, *Economic Trends*, July 1979, p. 16, inflated to 1978 prices using GDP index of total home costs. For comparability, nationalized industries' expenditure excluded from the official definition of public expenditure since 1976 has been reinstated. The figures are given by official statistics for calendar years.

Conservative. The passage of time explains 97 percent of the increase in public spending through the two decades, leaving very little to be explained by parties winning and losing office. In effect, time symbolizes the total effect of several inertia influences: demographic changes leading to an increase in spending on education, health and old age pensions; secular trends in the economy, such as rising unemployment increasing total spending on unemployment benefits; and, not least, the extra revenue generated for government by the fiscal dividend of economic growth.[7]

Each year, on an average £2.2 billion (in 1978 prices) has been added to total spending on public policies. In short, a newly elected Labour government can claim "credit" among Socialists for adding upwards of £10 billion to public spending in a given Parliament, even though inertia forces mean that this much extra spending was already in the pipeline. A Conservative government that, in the life of a Parliament, could keep the increase in public spending to £5 billion in constant terms would be doing much better than par for the course, reducing the average rate of increase by one-half. A government that actually achieved a cut of a billion pounds in the life of a Parliament would have achieved a heroic victory, effectively reversing a tide that otherwise would increase expenditure by more than £10 billion in constant terms.

One reason for the growth of public expenditure is that government grows with the economy as a whole. As the national product increases, there is more tax revenue to spend on public services; and people wish better roads for their new cars, rising pensions to keep in line with higher wages and better schools and health care. The ratio of public expenditure to the national product is a familiar indicator of the relationship between the two. From economic policy statements of the parties, the ratio would be expected to increase under a Labour government and remain constant or decline under a Conservative government. This could happen notwithstanding a steady upward trend in total public spending due to a difference between the parties in achieving economic growth.

In practice, the growth of public expenditure as a proportion of the gross domestic product has followed a secular trend upwards irrespective of the party in office. On the historic Treasury basis of accountancy, it rose from 41 percent in 1957 to 44 percent in the final year of that Conservative government. It then rose to 50 percent by the end of the 1964–70 Labour government and to 57 percent by the time the Heath government's policies had had full impact in 1974. The Wilson-Callaghan government exercised stronger controls on public spending—but only after it reached a record of 59 percent of the national product in 1975.[8]

The growth of public expenditure as a proportion of the national product reflects a secular trend. The relative importance of public expenditure increased in six of the seven years of the 1957–64 Conservative government and in all but one year of the Heath administration. Public expenditure's share of the national product has been rolled back only three times, all under Labour governments. The steadiness of the rise in public expenditure as a proportion of the national product is shown by the fact that inertia trend forces explain 87 percent of the increase.[9] On average, public spending has taken an extra 0.78 percent of the national product each year from 1957 to 1979, the equivalent of an extra 4 percent of the national product during the life of a Parliament—whether Conservative or Labour dominated.

While public expenditure has increased in total whether there is a Conservative or Labour government in office, total figures are only half the story of public expenditure. The other half concerns spending upon individual government programmes. Public spending can grow steadily in aggregate, but there can nonetheless be major differences in the growth rates of the individual programmes that collectively add up to the total of public expenditure.

When public expenditure is divided into more than a dozen major programme headings, the same basic pattern emerges: a secular trend upward in spending on the great majority of specific programmes. In *current* money terms, spending rose in 14 of 16 programme headings under the 1957–64 Conservative government, in all 16 headings under the 1964–70 Labour government and its 1970–74 Conservative successor and in 14 of the 16 major programme areas of the 1974–79 Labour government.[10]

When the effect of inflation is taken into account, there is still a secular trend up in *constant* price spending on nearly every major programme of British government. This trend appears regardless of whether the Conservative or Labour Party is in power (see table 7.1). From 1957 to 1964, spending rose on 15 of 17 major programmes of the Conservative government. Under the 1964–70 Labour government, spending also rose in 14 of 17 programme categories, a proportion that was matched by the Conservative government of Edward Heath. Spending rose less under the second Labour government, but still went up in 12 of 17 programmes.

The relatively few occasions when particular programmes were cut do not appear to reflect any partisan bias. The fact that more cuts occurred under Labour can readily be interpreted as an accident of timing: it was in office in the unusually difficult economic period of 1974–79. Of

TABLE 7.1 *Increases in Public Expenditure by Programme, 1957–78*

Programmes (in order of size, 1978)	Expenditure Constant 1978 £mn		Total % Change 1957–78	Annual Average % Rate of Change			
	1957	1978		1957–64 %	1964–70 %	1970–73 %	1973–78 %
Social security benefits	4,781	15,786	+230	+ 6.5	+ 5.7	+ 3.6	+ 6.3
Education	3,112	8,658	+178	+ 7.1	+ 5.6	+ 6.7	+ 0.8
National Health Service	2,932	7,615	+160	+ 4.6	+ 4.9	+ 5.3	+ 4.3
Military defence	6,895	7,287	+ 8	+ 0.3	− 1.3	+ 2.7	+ 0.6
Housing	2,012	5,073	+152	+ 5.3	+ 2.6	+11.7	+ 0.7
Industry and Trade including employment services	2,397	3,573	+ 49	+ 4.9	+ 8.5	+ 3.3	− 3.2
Roads, transport and communications	2,183	2,848	+ 30	+ 6.0	+ 5.8	+ 3.9	− 5.6
Environmental services	1,156	2,503	+116	+ 7.5	+ 5.8	+ 9.2	− 4.3
Law, order and protective services	625	2,391	+283	+ 9.5	+ 6.0	+ 7.5	+ 3.4
External relations	552	1,969	+257	+ 7.7	− 0.8	+14.7	+ 8.4
Personal social services	201	1,390	+591	+ 7.1	+14.4	+14.5	+ 5.4
Agriculture, forestry, fishing, food	1,464	999	− 32	− 3.0	− 1.8	− 0.7	− 1.5
Research	240	531	+121	+10.6	+ 3.9	− 2.9	− 2.2
School meals, milk, welfare foods	364	463	+ 27	+ 1.5	+ 2.2	− 2.9	+ 2.1
Libraries, museums and arts	94	392	+317	+ 8.3	+ 7.3	+12.6	+ 2.5
Other public services	899	1,326	+ 47	− 1.4	+ 6.9	+ 3.4	+ 1.6
Debt interest	4,066	8,341	+105	+ 2.4	+ 2.8	+ 2.7	+ 4.5
TOTAL	£33,970	£71,351	+110%	+ 4.2	+ 4.2	+ 5.0	+ 2.2

SOURCES: *National Income and Expenditure 1968* T53; 1979 ed. T9.4. 1957 and 1973 data inflated to 1978 prices using GDP index of total home costs. Annual rates of change 1957–73 from R. Klein, "The Politics of Public Expenditure," *British Journal of Political Science*6, no. 4 (1976): 412.

the thirteen cuts, four reflect a continuing downward trend in food sub-sidies under successive Conservative and Labour governments. The 1964 Labour government succeeded in cutting defence spending, but this cannot be regarded as an ideological victory, given the long-term decline in British military commitments, a decline started under its Conserva-tive predecessor. The cut with a clearest policy relevance was the down-turn in spending on school meals in the Heath government, achieved as a conscious act of policy by Mrs. Thatcher as Secretary of State for Edu-cation.[11]

The most noteworthy variation in the growth of public spending concerns the *relative rate at which spending* on individual programmes *increases*. Programmes grow at different rates under different govern-ments; the overall pattern emphasizes secular trends rather than con-flicting partisan intentions as the chief determinant of public spending. When the rate of increase in public spending by programmes among suc-cessive Conservative and Labour governments is compared, there is no consistent partisan pattern.

There are more programme areas in which the Conservatives con-sistently increased spending faster than Labour, if only because spending grew so much more slowly under the 1974–79 Labour government than under any of its predecessors. Conservatives increased spending more on education and housing, notwithstanding the fact that these are welfare services, which Labour likes to talk about. The Conservatives also in-creased spending more than Labour in two policy areas especially iden-tified with the party: defence and law and order. In the two decades, there are only two programme areas in which Labour consistently increased spending more than the Conservatives. The first—the provision of school meals and welfare foods—reflects a distinctive Labour policy concern. The second—payment of debt interest—does not.

Overall, the average annual rates of change reported in table 7.1 confirm the importance of secular trends rather than partisan policy pri-orities. The biggest shift in spending programmes occurred in the 1970s when the world economic conditions forced the Labour government, notwithstanding its predispositions, to reduce the rate of spending in-crease in constant terms below that of its Conservative predecessor for thirteen of the government's seventeen major programmes.

The launching of new programmes is the most dramatic way in which public expenditure can be influenced. A new measure not only makes initial claims upon the public purse but also implies a continually growing claim. The government of the day can also make long-term differences in the pattern of public expenditure by terminating rather than merely squeezing existing programmes. Differences in party economic doctrines imply more programmes started under a Labour government, and more established programmes abolished under a Conservative government.

Since 1970 annual Public Expenditure White Papers provide a clear and reasonably consistent basis for reviewing the inititation and termination of programme expenditure. The evidence of the 1970s rejects the conventional Adversary view of Labour as the party of new programmes and the Conservatives as a party abolishing expensive programmes. More new major spending programmes (16) were started under the 1970–74 Conservative government than under the 1974–79 Labour government (8). In a complementary manner, three programmes were abolished by the Labour government, and only one was terminated by its Conservative predecessor. [12]

The Heath government launched six new programmes, each costing more than £100 million by the end of its term of office. They were programmes to refinance fixed-rate export credits, invalidity benefits, compensating nationalized industries for price restraints, regional development grants, price supports under the Community Agricultural Policy and contributions to the European Community. By comparison, Labour launched only one programme—the Scottish and Welsh Development agencies—intended to cost more than £100 million by the end of its term of office in 1979. Three programmes each cost more than £100 million annually when first launched—food subsidies, the National Enterprise Board and British Rail grants—but each had its authorized spending cut heavily by 1979.

The impetus given to public spending by the 1970–74 Conservative government meant that its new programmes accounted for 4.4 percent of total public expenditure in the final year of the Heath administration. By comparison, the new programmes of the 1974–79 Labour government accounted for only 0.8 percent of total public expenditure in its final year. Moreover, unlike the Heath government, the additional cost of new Labour programmes could be more than offset by savings from programmes it had abolished. The three programmes abolished by Labour—compensation for nationalized industries' price restraint, the regional employment premium and sterling area guarantees—were costing slightly above £1 billion when the 1974 Labour government entered office.

Consensus in launching new spending programmes is demonstrated by the limited number of Adversary votes in the Commons in opposition to legislation authorizing additional claims upon the public purse. Labour voted against only three of the sixteen Conservative measures to find new ways of spending money, and the Conservatives against only half of the eight Labour measures.

The analysis of programme expenditure illustrates the importance of secular trends. Secular trends are important because the inertia forces of established programmes account for nearly all the growth in public spending. Programme headings on the Treasury books before the 1970 Conservative government entered office accounted for more than 95 percent of all spending by the Heath government at the time it left office. In the case of the Wilson-Callaghan government, already established programmes, with their inertia growth, accounted for 99 percent of total expenditure of the last year of that Labour administration. Inertia pressures to increase spending for established programmes affect the government of the day, whether Conservative or Labour.

Since public expenditure reflects many pressures outside the control of any party, no government can expect its actual expenditure to match exactly its announced spending intentions. On the basis of party doctrines, a Labour government would spend more than predicted, and a Conservative government would spend less. Such a pattern of "overshooting" and "undershooting" would be consistent with the Adversary model of party government.

The processes for managing public expenditure in Britain provide an excellent test of the extent to which parties differ in realizing their published spending intentions. Since 1966, each Public Expenditure White Paper has contained a government statement of spending intentions for up to five years ahead. These intentions are far more weighty than statements in party manifestos, for they are intentions backed up by the full force of the Treasury, which is responsible for their enforcement as well as their preparation.[13]

In practice, both Labour and Conservative governments have had a poor record of realizing their spending intentions, but there is no evidence of a partisan bias. If anything, the pattern resembles a random walk.[14] From 1966 to 1970 the Labour government allowed public spending to rise almost twice as much as it intended in constant price terms. The 1970–74 Conservative government was even more out of line; public expenditure grew more than three times what was intended (cf. table 7.1). The 1974–79 Labour government was the only one to err on the side of underspending. It forecast a larger growth in public spending than actually occurred. Its "cash limits" policy, adopted to combat inflation, resulted in public spending up to 1979 growing only one-quarter of what was initially forecast in 1975.

The technocratic capability of government is limited, to say the least, when it cannot even forecast, let alone control, the rate at which its own spending changes over a period of four years, and the errors are the opposite of the party's own political predispositions. Equally, the evidence shows the inability of the Treasury to sustain any fixed policy for a period of time, let alone a policy producing consensus benefits. There is a secular trend determined by forces greater than government can control or anticipate.

Economic Outcomes

From an individual citizen's point of view, the most important economic indicators are economic results; the inputs of public policy reviewed in the foregoing pages are but means to secure desirable outcomes. Since the policy inputs of parties in office have been primarily determined by secular trends, it would be expected that the overall performance of the British economy since 1957 owes more to long-term secular trends than to the policies of successive Conservative and Labour governments. The evidence reviewed in detail in this section shows that this is the case.

The growth of the gross domestic product is the single most important indicator of the national economy. This summary measure of the size of the nation's total resources shows how much in total is at hand to finance public expenditure and individual take-home pay. A technocrat would expect growth rates to vary little with the colour of the party in office. In a competitive party system, whatever politicians were in office, any group would try hard to do all that it could to make the economy grow. Conceivably, competition could lead to a virtuous cycle of ever higher growth rates. Alternatively, a committed Socialist or enthusiast for free enterprise would expect the national product to fluctuate in its course, differing with the Adversary policies of Labour and Conservative governments.

The record of economic growth since 1957 refutes the Adversary model of economic management. The switch from Conservative to Labour governments and back again has not been followed by a reversal in growth rates. Instead, it has been accompanied by a trend down in the annual average adjusted growth rate of the British economy under suc-

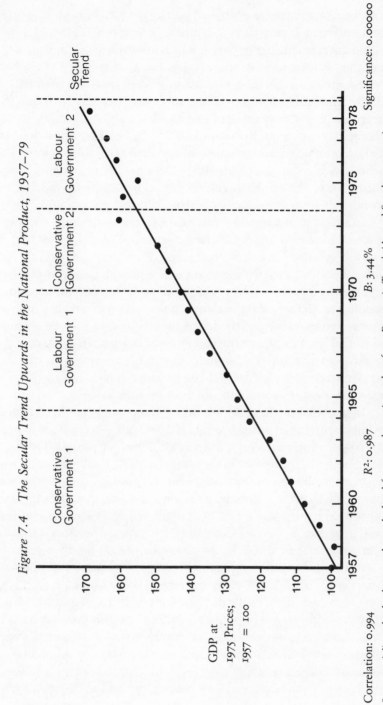

Figure 7.4   The Secular Trend Upwards in the National Product, 1957–79

Correlation: 0.994 R^2: 0.987   B: 3.44%   Significance: 0.00000

SOURCE: Adjusted calendar year data calculated for gross domestic product from *Economic Trends* (Annual Supplement 1979), p. 5.

cessive governments irrespective of party. The economy grew on average faster under the Macmillan government (2.6 percent) than under the first Wilson government (2.2 percent), which in turn had a higher growth rate than the Heath administration (1.4 percent). Growth was further depressed under the Wilson-Callaghan government (1.1 percent). The slump in the British economy under successive Conservative and Labour governments in the 1970s is not so much a sign of deterioration in the economic capacities of British politicians, but of a secular worsening in world economic conditions. Britain's growth rate, already low by comparison with its major competitors, dropped by nearly half from the Macmillan to the Heath government and by half from the first to the second Labour government of Harold Wilson.

In the past two decades successive Conservative and Labour governments have also faced a cyclical dilemma. Policies promoting economic growth also have their costs. No government, whatever its party, has been prepared to pay these costs for a period as long as the life of a Parliament. Hence, in each period of party government, the growth of the economy accelerates and then slows down, often reversing from year to year or even more frequently. In the 1957–64 Conservative government, the annual growth rate of the economy went through four reversals; in the 1964–70 Labour government, four more reversals; in the shorter Heath government, it changed course three times; and in the Wilson 1974–79 Labour government, three more reversals.[16]

In one respect, the secular trend in the economy has been benign; in the long term, the national product has been growing, and growing substantially through the years, even after allowance is made for inflation (see figure 7.4). The decline in the annual rate of growth has not normally meant an absolute contraction in the economy; it has simply meant slower growth in the economy. The larger the economy, the more money is produced in absolute terms by a small percentage increase in the national product. A 1 percent increase in the national product is equivalent to an additional £150 for the average four-person family a year.

In total, the national product increased by more than two-thirds from 1957 to 1979. Because any increase in the national product is good news, the government of the day is always ready to take credit for it. But the evidence displayed in figure 7.4 shows that this credit is hardly deserved. The increase has occurred under successive Conservative and Labour governments. So steady (if not steep) has been the secular trend up in economic growth that it can explain 98 percent of the total growth, independent of the policies of Conservative and Labour governments.

The chief departure from the trend—the surge in the economy in 1973, followed by the contraction in 1974–75—is in a period that neither party would like to recall with pride.

A growing national product can benefit citizens in two different and not necessarily conflicting ways. It can increase individual take-home pay, and it can increase public expenditure on such benefits as health, education and pensions. If the economic conditions are right, it can finance growth in both private and public affluence. It has already been shown that neither governing party has been able to cut spending on the provision of public policies (see figure 7.3). Therefore, at most the parties would be expected to differ in the priority given to increasing take-home pay. The differences between the two parties would be a matter of degree rather than kind; neither party would be expected to desire a *cut* in take-home pay.

In the past two decades, take-home pay has risen significantly and fairly steadily. From 1957 through 1978, the average industrial earnings of a married man with two children increased by 36 percent in constant value after paying taxes and adding in family allowances and child benefit. Within the lifetime of each governing party, there is a cyclical movement up and down in take-home pay. Under the 1957–64 Conservative government, the annual direction of take-home pay was reversed four times; under the 1964–70 Labour government, it reversed twice; under the 1970–74 Conservative government, once; and three times under the 1974–79 Labour government. Fluctuations in earnings not only reflect fluctuations in the national economy but also fluctuations in the governing party's attitude to enforcing an incomes policy. When an incomes policy is effective, wages tend to rise slowly if at all, because its introduction usually follows a period when the rise of money wages has far outstripped the increase in the national product. Wage rates tend to escalate regularly, Professor H. A. Turner explains, in the run up to a general election, when the governing party loosens restraints upon wages for fear that otherwise it will lose votes. This happened very noticeably in 1964, 1970, 1974 and 1979. In each case it was followed by a period of inflation, thus depressing real money wages.[17]

In the long term, take-home pay is more subject to secular trends than party differences. Figure 7.5 demonstrates that over the two decades as a whole, there has been a clear upward trend in take-home pay, accounting for 86 percent of the total increase. Take-home pay grew more under the 1957–64 Conservative government (16 percent) than under the first Wilson government (10 percent), and also more under

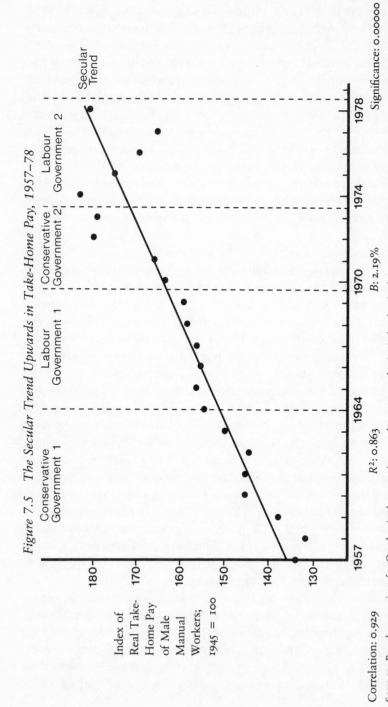

Figure 7.5 *The Secular Trend Upwards in Take-Home Pay, 1957–78*

Correlation: 0.929   R²: 0.863   B: 2.19%   Significance: 0.00000

SOURCE: Based on earnings for October in the year given, and tax rate and price index for the financial year. House of Commons *Hansard* Written Answers 22 July 1977 (vol. 935, col. 773); 6 June 1978 (vol. 951, col. 131); 1978 adjusted in light of actual earnings and prices in October 1978 from *Department of Employment Gazette* (August 1979), pp. 836 and 846.

the Heath government (10 percent) than under the 1974–79 Labour government (1 percent). Within this time span, there appear to be two very different movements. The first is a steady trend *up* in take-home pay from the 1950s to 1971; secular forces, independent of party, account for 94 percent of the total change. Since 1972, there has been a trend *down* in take-home pay. Take-home pay has fallen in four of six years to October 1978, rising only in preelection booms. The downturn has occurred under both Conservative and Labour governments. It is not a conscious object of policy but an incidental (and unwanted) byproduct of a relatively rapid growth in public expenditure and a relatively slow growth in the national product.

The distribution of income is politically important, whatever the state of the national economy, for Socialists proclaim that they favour the equalization of income, whereas Conservatives believe that differences in income are socially and economically natural and desirable. The more parlous the state of the economy, the more these differences might be expected to become important, since there is not a large enough fiscal dividend of growth to provide something for everybody.

A straightforward measure of the distribution of income is the proportion of earnings in the hands of the top half of the population, after taking taxes into account.[19] This would be expected to fall under Labour governments because of that party's professed egalitarian outlook, and rise, or at least remain constant, under a Conservative government. Such a cyclical trend would be electorally reasonable, for the Conservatives draw a disproportionate amount of their vote from people earning above-average wages, and Labour from those earning below-average wages.

In practice, the strongest influence upon the distribution of earnings appears to be a secular trend toward greater equality (or less inequality) in earnings (see figure 7.6). From 1961 to 1976, the period for which the best evidence is available, the distribution of income has tended to narrow, whichever party is in office. The trend down is small, averaging 0.1 percent annually, but it is statistically significant, and the secular trend can explain 57 percent of the change. There are substantial fluctuations around the broad overall trend toward income equalization. This would be expected, for neither Conservative nor Labour governments have had explicit policies to equalize incomes. Changes in the distribution of income are often the byproduct of technocratic policies adopted in pursuit of other objectives (e.g., a wages policy or incentives to investment) or reflect larger changes in the economy as a whole.

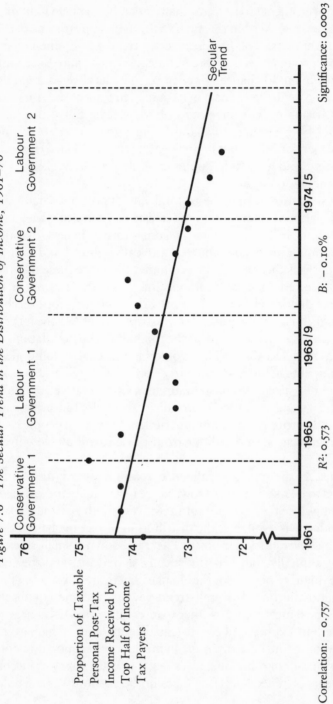

Figure 7.6   The Secular Trend in the Distribution of Income, 1961–76

Correlation: – 0.757   R²: 0.573   B: – 0.10%   Significance: 0.0003

SOURCE: Royal Commission on the Distribution of Income and Wealth, Report 7 (London: HMSO, Cmnd. 7595), table A.3; Calendar year data, 1961–67; financial year, 1968/69–1976/77.

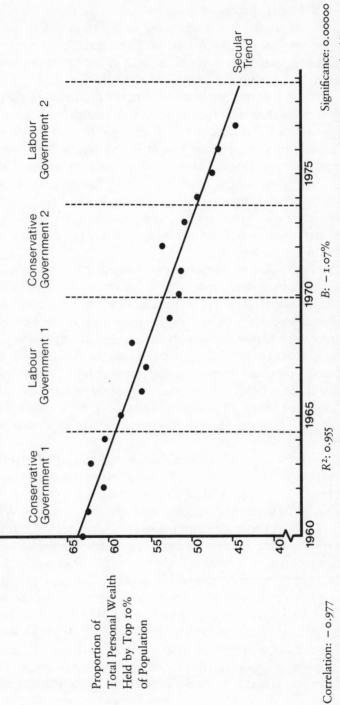

Figure 7.7   The Secular Trend in the Distribution of Wealth, 1960–77

Correlation: – 0.977   R²: 0.955   B: – 1.07%   Significance: 0.0000

SOURCE: 1960–73, Royal Commission on the Distribution of Income and Wealth, Report 1 (London: HMSO, Cmnd. 6171), table 45; 1974–77, Inland Revenue Statistics 1979 (London: HMSO), table 4.19 (calendar years).

A second major test of egalitarianism is the distribution of wealth. People with capital are much more secure than individuals with the same income but no capital at hand. Here again, a Labour government would be expected to reduce differences in wealth, and a Conservative government to maintain or increase them.

There is a significant trend toward the reduction of inequalities in wealth, as measured by the proportion of wealth held by the top tenth of British society (see figure 7.7). From 1960 to 1977 the proportion of wealth held by the top 10 percent of society has declined from 63 to 44 percent. The trend down has occurred under successive Conservative and Labour governments; the direction of change has occasionally reversed under governments of each party because the distribution of wealth can be a byproduct of other policies. But the secular trend is both clear and strong. It accounts for 95 percent of the redistribution of wealth in the period.

Since 1945, the only economic goals equal in importance to economic growth have been the maintenance of full employment and stable prices. During this period, economists have assumed that there is usually a relationship between the two: A government can choose between having less inflation and more unemployment or less unemployment and more inflation. The economic doctrines and interests of the two parties imply that successive Conservative and Labour governments would make Adversary choices. Under a Conservative government, inflation would fall, and under a Labour government, unemployment would fall and inflation rise.[21] The long-term result would be differing choices when confronted with a dilemma.

In practice, unemployment has shown a secular trend upwards under successive Conservative and Labour governments in the past two decades. In the 1957–64 Macmillan government, unemployment averaged 2.0 percent; it was virtually the same under the first Wilson government, 2.1 percent. Unemployment rose during the Heath administration, averaging 3.2 percent annually, and under the second Labour government it rose further still, averaging 5.2 percent.

At a quick glance, the graphic display of unemployment trends in figure 7.8 might suggest that British government enjoys the luxury of a dilemma choice, for unemployment has fallen as well as risen in the period of each party in power. But careful analysis shows that the secular trend is stronger. Throughout the two decades, it accounts for 64 percent of the total variation in unemployment, with unemployment increasing on average at a rate of 0.9 percent in the five-year life of a Par-

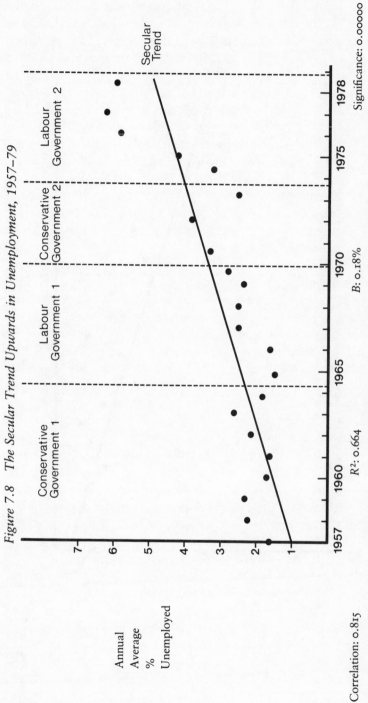

Figure 7.8   The Secular Trend Upwards in Unemployment, 1957–79

Correlation: 0.815 R^2: 0.664   B: 0.18%   Significance: 0.00000

SOURCES: British Labour Statistics Historical Abstract (HMSO, 1971), table 168; Department of Employment Gazette, July 1979, p. 698.

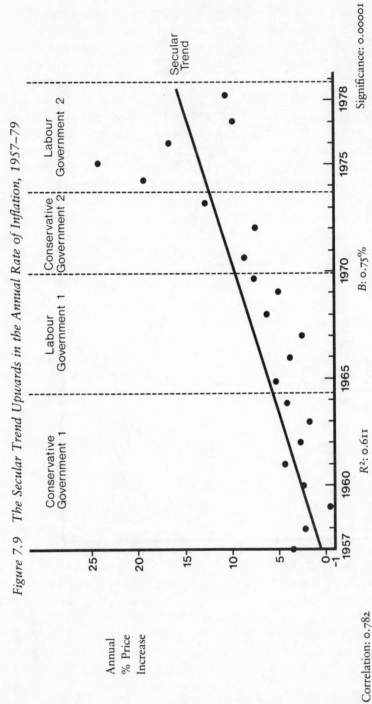

Figure 7.9   The Secular Trend Upwards in the Annual Rate of Inflation, 1957–79

Correlation: 0.782   R²: 0.611   B: 0.75%   Significance: 0.0001

SOURCES: *British Labour Statistics Historical Abstract* (HMSO, 1971), table 95/96; *Department of Employment Gazette*, July 1979, p. 726. Adjusted calendar years.

liament. The difference in the average level of employment from 1957 to 1970, and in the 1970s, emphasizes the importance of secular forces stronger than the governing party, for the rising level of unemployment has affected both Conservative and Labour governments in the 1970s.[22]

Just as Labour governments have been forced to ride a trend upwards in unemployment against their own strongly held wishes, so too Conservative governments have been forced to preside over a steady increase in rates of inflation. The average annual rate of inflation has shown a secular trend upwards through two decades. In the 1957–64 Conservative government, prices increased on average 2.5 percent annually. In the 1964–70 Labour government, the annual rate of price increase was 4.9 percent. In the 1970–74 Heath administration, inflation was 9.4 percent annually, and in the 1974–79 Labour government, prices increased annually by an average of 15.1 percent. In short, the data refute the Adversary model of inflation reversing when the party controlling government changes hands.

Inflation has been growing annually and cumulatively since 1957. The force of the secular trend upwards is shown in figure 7.9. More than half the rate of increase (61 percent) can be accounted for by the passage of time. On average, each year prices tend to *increase 0.7 percent more* than the increase of the year before. In other words, a party entering office with an inflation rate of 5 percent would be likely to leave it five years later with an inflation rate of 9 percent, regardless of its partisan colour.

All six measures of the state of the economy point to the same conclusion: the preeminence of secular trends, whatever the party in power. In each case, the continuing trend explains more than half of all the change, and in three cases, five-sixths or more of changes in the state of the economy.

The Force of Circumstance

The management of the economy by successive Conservative and Labour governments through the years is a standing refutation of any simple belief in technocratic government. The best and brightest minds in the civil service have applied themselves to the problems of the British economy, and many in universities have done so as well. So too have successive Chancellors of the Exchequer and Prime Ministers. The result has been disappointing at best and disturbing at worst. By almost every standard economic indicator, the condition of the British economy has worsened from 1957 to 1979; Britain has one of the poorer and weaker economies of Europe.

Nor has there been any consensus among economists about how to put the economy to rights. When economists are faced with an immediate and important political issue where their professional knowledge is relevant, they often disagree. Nor is it an accident that disagreements occur along party lines, for economists are not value-free observers of natural phenomena. They are strongly and sometimes passionately committed to values and premises derived from a perfectly legitimate and serious civic concern with major problems of society. The results can nonetheless be frustrating to anyone expecting consensus among experts about what to do. For example, in 1971 when Britons were hotly debating whether to enter the Common Market and economic arguments were in the forefront of debate, an opinion poll was conducted to ascertain the views of economists. The result was complete dissensus: 40 percent favoured entry and 42 percent were against. The median economist was literally a "don't know."[23]

Even with hindsight, British economists find it impossible to agree among themselves about how the economy should have been managed. In 1977, the National Institute of Economic and Social Research demonstrated how great the disagreements are by inviting four different teams of economists to analyze retrospectively the nation's economic problems as of September 1964, just prior to the Labour government's entry to office; July 1970, when the Conservatives entered office; and looking forward to the problems up to the end of 1981. The contending teams were identified with different political as well as economic tendencies — on the farthest left, the Cambridge Economic Policy group, and then the more orthodox Keynesian National Institute, and to the right of centre, the London Business School and an outright monetarist, David Laidler. The results demonstrated the empirical limitations of theoretically sophisticated, quantitative and computerized econometric models. One of their number, Charles Goodhart, concluded from the deliberations:

> What comes out of all this I fear is that models cannot give much help to policy makers. Looking at exactly the same economy, and even using on occasions very similar structural equations, different modellers come to totally different policy conclusions because of their fundamental perceptions about the working of the economy.

Econometrics has not, at least so far, provided any alternative for basic judgment, only some quantitative dressing and support for such judgments.[24]

Neither sophisticated intelligence nor determined ignorance has been capable of directing the economy along lines that both Conservative and Labour leaders agree are desirable. Secular forces stronger than politicians and economists put together have been the principal determinant of the state of the British economy since 1957. This point is demonstrated by the fact that, statistically, in all nine graphic tests in this chapter a significant secular trend was found, which on average explains 75 percent of the total change in the period. Social scientists disagree about the causes of these trends. The point demonstrated here is the relative weakness of party politicians and, for that matter, social scientists seeking to give direction to government.

Unfortunately, the forces driving the British economy are driving it in the wrong direction. Before entering office, Conservative and Labour politicians make a plenitude of statements about what they will do to "get the economy right." After leaving office, they and their supporters have a plenitude of explanations about why it was not as easy as expected to do what they wished.[25] Whether the initial intentions voiced are Consensual (e.g., to increase the rate of growth) or Adversary (e.g., to affect the distribution of income), the results tend to be the same. The momentum of the economy continues to determine inputs and outcomes, whether the Chancellor of the day seeks guidance from a Red or a Blue book.

The progress of the economy is not completely determined. There is an element of choice open to every government. This chapter shows that short-term changes do occur in the economy, notwithstanding long-term trends. The changes do not, however, conform to the normal Adversary model of party government. Instead, there are cycles of *change within* the life of a party in office. The governing party can try all available economic remedies in a grand tour of policies intended to improve an economy that is increasingly recalcitrant to treatment. But the changes are likely to appear small when measured in results. Whatever their scale, they are important to politicians as evidence of choices within a circumscribed field of manoeuvre. This is true even if the choice is simply which horn of the dilemma to approach first.

In the short run, politicians in office can try to exploit their room for manoeuvre, but not in the way predicted by Adversary economic ideologies. Instead, actions may reflect a Consensus: The most important thing about being in government is winning the next election. The governing party does not need to manage the economy well throughout its period of office; it should appear to be guiding the economy satisfactorily in the months leading up to a general election. Thanks to the power that a governing party has to determine the date of a general election, it need only generate a short-run improvement in the economy, or even wait until a random fluctuation makes conditions improve, to call an election when its chances of winning are on the rise too. At times, this strategy can work, as in 1959, 1966 or 1974—but success may then be followed by worsening economic conditions. Just as often, the economic record of the governing party is a major reason for its defeat.

Cumulatively, the effect of secular trends is to make the British economy progressively worse. An annual increase in the rate of inflation of a few percent may seem small, but when this compounds over two decades, it results in a several hundred percent increase in prices. Since 1957 the level of unemployment has increased almost four times, and the national product has grown but 67 percent. Successive governments have had to intensify their inputs of policy—pushing interest rates or government deficits higher—in an attempt to achieve the same results as earlier. *Greater effort* by government now threatens to be followed by *less success* than before. The proportion of economic bad news in Britain appears to be increasing regardless of the party in office.

In an oft quoted but fundamentally misleading epigram, Keynes said: "In the long run, we are all dead."[26] The statement is true of individuals, but not of economies. Every time a party enters office, it inherits the accumulated successes and failures of its predecessors. Social scientists may take some pleasure in developing theories to explain why the British economy has shown an increasing downward secular trend. But the continuing inability of either (or both) Conservative and Labour governments to overcome downward economic trends is bad news for party politicians struggling to exert their will against an economy that is increasingly difficult to manage. It is even worse news for citizens. It suggests that whether Mrs. Thatcher, Tony Benn or anyone else is in office in the 1980s, the problems of the British economy may become even worse than before.

CHAPTER 8

Something Stronger Than Parties

The short answer to the question posed in the title of this book is: Yes, parties do make a difference in the way Britain is governed—but the differences are not as expected. The differences in office between one party and another are less likely to arise from contrasting intentions than from the exigencies of government. Much of a party's record in office will be stamped upon it by forces outside its control. British parties are not the primary forces shaping the destiny of British society; it is shaped by something stronger than parties.

In the aristocratic past, individual politicians believed that they could make *all* the difference to the government of the country. Government was seen as a test of will, and the person with the strongest will could bend government or even the whole of society to his ends. In a British context, the idea of the "great man" influencing history was usually benign in intent. In Continental Europe, often it was not.

Contemporary government is impersonal, not personal. Too much writing about politics today is faulty because it ignores this fundamental fact. Because names make news and faces make television images, contemporary journalism concentrates on the personalities of politics as much as in an aristocratic age. But in doing so it loses sight of government itself, that is, the large agglomeration of complex bureaucracies that in practice carry out the work done in the name of Cabinet ministers.

Contemporary theories of representative government make parties doubly necessary: to offer the electorate a choice between competing teams of governors and to formulate policies that those elected can then carry out. To recognize the importance of parties is not to argue that parties are all-important in the government of Britain. Taken altogether, the Conservative and Labour parties are only part of the political system. While the fact of election gives the governing party a legitimacy denied many other groups, it does not *ipso facto* give it the power to do what it wishes.

In this concluding chapter, the first section evaluates the relative significance of models tested in preceding pages. The second section explains why the Adversary approach to party government does not hold, and the constraints that make Consensus dominate British government. The third section examines the dynamics of the Moving Consensus that effectively accounts for both continuity *and* change within the policy process. The final section uses the experience of the past two decades to throw light on the problems of party government in Britain in the 1980s.

The Models That Fit

At a given point in time, the Consensus model has best described party government in Britain. It provides the best description of how the Conservative and Labour parties contest election campaigns and how they act upon legislation in the House of Commons. The extent of Consensus politics is made most evident by what does *not* happen in the division lobbies of the House of Commons. The opposition usually does not vote against government bills, for many proposals of the governing party are generally agreed and the governing party exercises a measure of self-restraint in what it puts to the Commons.

British parties tend to behave in Consensus terms because they owe their position to popular election, and the British electorate tends towards agreement rather than disagreement on major issues. There is nothing inherent in the nature of the electoral system making both major parties tend towards agreement. If the electorate were polarized, then the parties would be Adversaries. In Northern Ireland the British electoral system (and subsequently, proportional representation) has not ended Adversary politics. Ulster parties must be Adversaries as long as the electorate that they represent is itself polarized.[1]

In no sense does the electorate dictate policies to parties, except in the atypical circumstances of a referendum. But the sanction of electoral defeat is sufficiently real and present to make politicians think twice before following ideological commitments likely to offend the great bulk of popular opinion. Those most sensitive to electoral currents tend to be among the parliamentary leaders of the parties. As long as popular support for the Conservative and Labour parties is relatively evenly divided and the electoral system magnifies relatively small swings in votes into a reversal of roles between government and opposition, frontbench MPs have every reason to be sensitive to the views of the electorate.

Because politics is by definition about the articulation of different opinions, there are always disagreements about what government ought to do. These differences must find some expression in the party system, as well as in the clashes of interest independent of parties. The fact that both parties yield to forces stronger than themselves does not mean that they are similar in all respects.

Parties are most ready to act as Adversaries when their own interests are immediately at stake. Politicians want to win, and they will therefore fight each other hard when proposals are put forward to change the electoral system or other rules of the game. Parties do not view the institutions of government as neutral technocratic instruments of "good government." A party that goes "too far" in pushing its own wishes when in office will be defenceless against a similar move from its opponents once they are in power. Prudent self-interest, if not goodwill, limits controversial changes in the rules of the game of Westminster politics.

Under certain limiting conditions, the parties can act as Adversaries, if each party considers itself particularly indebted to an identifiable group, and these groups disagree with each other about a particular set of policies. This is most evident in the annual discussions leading up to the Budget. The Confederation of British Industry and the Trades Union Congress differ about the apportionment of tax burdens, and some spending priorities. Equally important, most above-average taxpayers vote Conservative, and most paying less-than-average taxes vote Labour. Hence, at the margin a Conservative and Labour Chancellor would be expected to act somewhat differently in modifying taxes.

But the extent of Adversary interests can easily be exaggerated. For example, the Labour government sought to introduce trade union regulation in 1969, a forerunner of the 1971 Conservative legislation—and both met the same fate, frustration by the unions. In housing policy, the Conservatives receive the bulk (but not all) of votes from mortgage payers, and Labour the bulk of votes from council house tenants. But the Conservatives do not press for all council tenants to pay economic rents, nor has a Labour government sought to repeal tax relief for mortgage payers. Each party is more afraid of losing support where it is a minority than wishing to push interests and ideology to their conclusion.

The analysis of manifestos further underscores the limits of Adversary politics. Most of the things that parties say ought to be done are "do-able," and both Conservative and Labour governments in fact carry out most of their pledges. In the life of a Parliament, however, these measures constitute but a limited proportion of the activities of government; a substantial proportion of manifesto measures are accepted without a division in the Commons by the opposition.

The more carefully a manifesto is examined, the more sharply the distinction emerges between the policy-making role and its "preaching and teaching" role. At the level of rhetoric, individual politicians can say what they like in efforts to catch the headlines or sway the emotions of committed party stalwarts. Because controversy makes headline news, rhetorical statements by individual MPs can give the impression of two Adversary organizations. But this impression is false, because the individuals making such statements usually lack the endorsement of their party for what they say. The greater the gap between official party policy and what an individual proclaims, the more attention is given to Adversary politics *within* parties. Anthony Wedgwood Benn and Enoch Powell are the contemporary past masters of highlighting intra-party divisions.

A party's election manifesto is a bureaucratic rather than a rhetorical document. It cannot be reduced to headlines — though it may have an innocuous and appealing title — because it is an amalgam of specific proposals to deal with specific concerns of some twenty Whitehall departments. Stylistically, manifestos err on the side of dullness because the everyday work of government usually appears dull. Yet by the same token, dull statements of intent tend to be realistic, and can be enacted without the Adversary conflict of headline rhetoric.

As the years pass, the static appearance of Consensus is eroded by the dynamic force of secular trends. The record of Labour or Conservative governments a decade apart will not reproduce itself exactly, for the pressures on government do not stand still. The flux and, in the 1970s, the turbulence of the environment of public policy make it impossible for the party in office to repeat exactly what has been done in a previous Parliament, let alone what it had done in a previous term of office.

Secular trends arise from forces stronger than the wishes of the electorate or the will of any Cabinet minister. British government is itself but part of a system of institutions and processes that jointly determine public policies. Many forces outside government—social conditions, pressure group demands, climates of public opinion and journalistic fashion—also influence what the government of the day can and cannot choose to do. Even though a party may be nominally sovereign, British government is not all-powerful against the problems it faces. Great constraints upon action come with the job of being a Cabinet minister.

Secular trends exert strong pressures upon the governing party, but they are not deterministic or necessarily unidirectional. There is always some room for manoeuvre within the lifetime of a Parliament. For example, short-term and small-scale changes in economic inputs and outcomes are frequent and, if properly timed, can be crucial electorally. In terms of the difference that parties can make to society, the long-term trends are more important than short-term Adversary reversals. Whether trend forces are good or bad news, short-term or long-term, they are forces to which any party must adapt once in office.

The strength of secular trends is a reminder that it is naive to hope that technocratic knowledge can solve social and economic problems that are intrinsic to politics. At best, technology can provide a means of coping with these problems. This is particularly true of the management of the economy. Economic management presents a continuing series of choices to the government of the day. Chapter 7 shows how vain is the expectation of a technocratic means to direct the economy towards goals agreed by both parties, or to achieve priorities of either.

To emphasize the force of a relatively consensual electorate and powerful secular trends is *not* to assert that the beliefs and interests of Conservative and Labour politicians are identical. Similarity in behaviour need not imply an identity of values. It can occur in spite of underlying differences if the specifics of a given circumstance are sufficiently powerful to lead people with different perspectives to arrive at the same conclusion about what must be done. *Necessity more than ideological consensus is the explanation for similarities in behaviour.*

Votes Count, Resources Decide

While an election is important, it is not all-important. The tabulation of votes decides which party will govern for the life of a new Parliament. Electoral victory legitimates a party's claim to government. But the division of the vote emphasizes that the governing party does not represent everybody.

Whereas votes count, resources decide.[2] In any system of representative and responsible government, the party in office ought to be influenced by those who press demands upon it and by events that could not be foreseen before it takes office. A party is not put in power simply to do what it wants. It must also do what is necessary and what is broadly desirable and acceptable in society. Inevitably, differences of opinion arise about *what* is necessary and desirable. Yet a party in government can no more ignore that half of the nation that did not vote for it than it can please all the people all the time. Individuals and groups on the losing side in a general election still exercise very substantial power in society. As a Conservative committee chaired by Lord Carrington reported to Mrs. Thatcher about trade unions in 1978:

> The Conservatives could not, when next in government, ride off into the sunset and take everybody on. There was no magic available to Mrs. Thatcher, as there had been none for Mr. Heath.[3]

The bulk of the resources crucial to the success or failure of policies are not altered by a general election ballot. If they were, then every five years the electorate could vote for an assurance of peace and prosperity. In practice, the supporters of the governing party can expect to be disillusioned within a year or two of polling day. Cabinet ministers are uniquely placed to learn, and to learn quickly, that their popular mandate does not give them the resources to do all that they wish. It gives them full responsibility for the direction of a complex, mixed-economy welfare state. But ministers also find that electoral success brings them up against the constraints of office.

Ironically, the first constraint upon party government comes from within. Every party is an amalgam of groups with differing outlooks, and office introduces a new source of division. In opposition, party leaders are united in weakness with their followers. All can ignore the constraints of office. By contrast, a governing party is fundamentally divided into the party leaders inside Whitehall and the party "outside the gates." The potential for internal conflict is reduced insofar as the party rank and file has loyalty and pride in its leadership. But strains on loyalty will appear as soon as discrepancies arise between what the party's rank and file would like to see happen and what is done by its leaders in their name.

The constraints from within are greater for a Labour than for a Conservative government. One reason is institutional: The Labour Party gives greater weight to its extraparliamentary institutions of policy making than does the Conservative Party. The National Executive Committee, as well as the parliamentary leadership, has a hand in the preparation of an election manifesto. By contrast, in the Conservative Party the parliamentary leader is left considerable discretion to determine how much or how little weight the views of the extraparliamentary party should have. The second difference is the wider spectrum of political outlooks found within the Labour Party. The Labour left is opposed in principle and practice to Consensus government, and it has greater weight within Labour's ranks than the differing groups and tendencies forming the "right" of the Conservative Party at a given moment.[4]

The effect of internal divisions is to limit the extent (or the ease) with which a party in government can abandon or slip through the loopholes of manifesto commitments. The manifesto is an explicit statement of what the leaders are expected to do—and a statement in which the leadership has concurred. Because of remoteness from the influences of office, the extraparliamentary party is more likely to press for the accomplishment of all the pledges written into the manifesto than is the leadership of the governing party. Instead of counting what its leaders have done, the Labour left tends to concentrate on what it has not done and, according to the left, should have done.[5]

Party competition is the second major constraint upon the governing party, more than offsetting any internal party divisions encouraging Adversary policies. A party does not seek votes in isolation, however introverted its most ardent members may become. Instead, it must win votes in competition with other parties. A party can be as different as it wants from its competitors, and can introduce Adversary policies that emphasize its difference. But the electorate can penalize it for what is regarded as an aggressive display of stubbornness in persisting in a given course notwithstanding great controversy.

The process of party competition will lead towards Consensus when the differences within the electorate are fewer and weaker. As long as there is a clear majority view about an issue within the electorate—say, the desirability of remaining within the Western military alliance—then both parties are likely to endorse it. If parties are to represent the electorate, the major parties should differ only when there is clear evidence of majorities in their ranks differing from each other. These differences do occur, but they are not so frequent as party competition implies. Moreover, the large number of voters with no opinion or no strongly held opinion on a given issue allows considerable leeway to leaders.

In the abstract, a newly elected government could use its parliamentary majority to "rubber stamp" legislation for five years, whatever the party's resulting unpopularity with the electorate. However, no government has ever sought to ride out criticism from outside as well as within the House of Commons for so long a period. The reminders of electoral mortality are presented to an unpopular government whenever a by-election threatens. The prospect of electoral defeat makes MPs in marginal seats sensitive to the government's popularity, and may also demoralize ministers and backbenchers holding safe seats. Speculation about seeking a new leader to "stop the rot" further confuses the governing party.

To ignore immediate and palpable signs of electoral unpopularity is a course that no Prime Minister willingly risks, for a Prime Minister is (or should be) a party manager. To fail in this role is to lose all, as Edward Heath found out. The threat of defeat is usually sufficient to lead the governing party to alter its policies. A U-turn in policy is awkward because it involves a single extreme course of action. The art of alteration, as Bagehot long ago observed, is to interpolate the new reality within an ancient show.[6] Reciprocally, an extremely popular government exerts pressure on its chief competitor to adapt its programme to compete more effectively.

Entry into government is a third constraint. Parliamentary party leaders abruptly become aware of how limited is the part that party politics plays in the political system of Britain. Awareness is immediately thrust upon newly installed Cabinet ministers when they are presented by their civil servants with a list of immediately pressing problems facing their department. The problems were there before the election campaign started, and had they been easy to resolve, would have been resolved previously for the sake of electoral kudos. As a minister begins to read through files documenting the difficulties of his department, it becomes increasingly clear that "the honeymoon is over," that is to say, the days of enjoying policy making free from the responsibilities of office are no more.

Winning office makes party leaders into departmental ministers. Politicians no longer spend their days rubbing shoulders with fellow MPs, extraparliamentary supporters and constituents. Instead, their day is organized by their civil servants, and priority is normally given to their obligations as heads of large, bureaucratic government departments. Contacts are first and foremost with civil servants, not with partisan supporters. A good civil servant is meant to do a minister's bidding, but part of that job is to remind a minister of things that he might prefer not to know. In opposition, a minister could ignore obstacles to realizing party intentions. To ignore these obstacles in office would be to court disaster. Civil servants tend to be the institutional spokesmen for the obstacles.

When a minister attends meetings with "outsiders," that is, persons not in his ministry, he usually meets them as a departmental representative, and not as a party spokesman. After nineteen years as a Labour Party politician, Barbara Castle found herself in Cabinet and learned to her surprise: "I wasn't in a political caucus at all. I was faced by departmental enemies."[7] When pressure group representatives meet the minister, he must be particularly on guard against agreeing with requests for the sake of being agreeable, for this would be taken as a government commitment. Commitments cannot be given by a minister without the assurance of backing by the Cabinet. The same is true when demands are voiced by backbench colleagues of the minister.

Whereas an opposition leader can confine discussions about policy to groups congenial to the party (e.g., trade unions *or* business), a minister is faced with conflicting demands from *both* sets of groups. The experience of these conflicting pressures is likely to alter a minister's idea of what a party can do when it is responsible for governing the whole of the country. The "other side's" pressure groups and groups that keep a foot in both parties must be given serious consideration when their cooperation is needed for the success of a government policy. The more important the policy, for example, a major decision about the economy, the more likely the government is to require the cooperation of both trade unions and business groups.

Global politics is the fourth and ultimate constraint upon the actions of any party governing Britain. While a newly elected government expects its own institutions to respond to its new directions, the rest of the world does not have to treat Britain any differently simply because a new government has taken office. Foreign countries tend to be neutral about the domestic politics of Britain; they are prepared to do business with any government that the British electorate might conceivably choose. But the indifference of the rest of the world becomes a handicap when the success of a government measure, say, a desire to reduce imports, requires the cooperation of other nations. Moreover, the pursuit of national self-interest by other countries makes life difficult for the government of the day in London.

Any party governing Britain is particularly subject to international constraints in its most important contemporary task, managing the economy. While successive British governments have taken more powers over the national economy since 1945, the British economy has concurrently become increasingly subject to international economic conditions beyond the control of Britain, or for that matter, the government of any nominally sovereign state. It is arguable that the most important determinants of the direction of the British economy today are the decisions made in other countries. These decisions cause changes in imports and exports, fluctuations in the value of the pound and changes in the world price of such basic commodities as oil.

During the decades reviewed here, the line conventionally separating international politics from domestic politics has been so blurred that in some places it has become obliterated. Economic issues have replaced military security as the everyday stuff of international politics. While national security remains important, it is only contingently of concern. By contrast, economic conditions are continuously pressing, for the daily flow of money in and out of the City of London affects the exchange rate of sterling, and all major economic indicators are monitored on a monthly or quarterly basis. Changes in the international economy can cause changes — for better or worse — in the British economy, and changes in the British economy influence the country's international trading position with consequences feeding back to domestic policy. For example, the international pressures leading to the devaluation of the pound in 1969 or Britain seeking a loan from the International Monetary Fund in 1976 forced the government to adopt policies that had a substantial and unwanted short-term effect on the Labour government's spending plans and its electoral popularity.

Britain's membership in the European Community is the most obvious symbol of constraint upon a British government's powers of decision. Treaty obligations bind it to accept decisions jointly agreed within the Community and not to adopt policies that contravene Community obligations. Membership in the Commonwealth imposes few juridical obligations, but Britain's influence there depends upon frequent consultation, and respect for views of valued Commonwealth partners. The special relationship with America appears to have declined in political significance, but Britain remains significantly influenced by the ups and downs of the American economy. For the time being at least, the British government incidentally benefits from OPEC policies that raise the world price of oil, including that of Britain's North Sea oil.

Ironically, the farther one gets from Westminster, the more obvious the constraints upon British government become. Roy Jenkins gave expression to this sentiment in a 1979 lecture aptly titled "Home Thoughts from Abroad":

> We must try to lengthen our perspective and escape from the tyranny of the belief, against all the evidence, that one government can make or break us....
>
> A governing party must have the self-confidence to want power and to believe that its exercise of it can tilt the country in the right direction. But it should also have the humility to recognise that, on any likely projection of the past, its power will come to an end, probably in about six years. The test of its statesmanship, in the context of history, will not therefore be how many trees it pulls up by the roots, but how it fits into a continuous process of adaptation in which leadership is combined with sensitivity to national mood.[8]

The sentiments are not those of a missionary for the market economy or a builder of a Socialist Jerusalem. According to taste, they could be characterized as Whiggish or Fabian, because of their emphasis on both continuity and change.

The Dynamics of a Moving Consensus

The record of party government in Britain from 1957 to 1979 rejects a "big bang" theory of parties making all the difference to Britain's government, let alone to society at large. But the record also shows that there are many *particular* differences in the way in which parties approach political problems and in the specific content and timing of a substantial amount of legislation. It is impossible to say that these differences are small, for this begs the question: How much of a difference is enough? From the viewpoint of practicing politicians, the differences that parties can make are important. The margin for change, whatever size it is, is regarded as 100 percent of the action that government can effect.

The best way to evaluate the impact of parties is to view their actions across a span of several Parliaments, instead of the momentary confrontation in the House of Commons or a single general election. In the course of two decades, both Conservative and Labour parties have had a chance to show what they do when given the power to govern Britain; about one-third of today's laws were enacted in the period under review here. The record of party government through the years emphasizes both continuity and change.

Viewed in a long-term perspective, party government in Britain is best characterized by the dynamics of a Moving Consensus. Movement can come from differences in the priorities of the parties and the disagreements thus generated. Equally, it can come from a Conservative or Labour government responding to secular trends by taking Consensus initiatives. When one party moves, it may occupy a position that has also been endorsed by its opponents—even if its opponents have since moved on to advocate other policies.

Paradoxically, the process begins when one of the parties breaks the consensus view that "everything is all right" in a given policy area.[9] It may do so in opposition, voicing a demand for action, or in office, requesting civil servants to prepare plans for draft legislation. Either the Conservative or Labour Party can take the initiative to put an issue on the agenda of public policy. Moreover, it can take the initiative unilaterally, without regard to the views of its opponents. Often, a major issue is broached in stages. It is first put forward by an interested group within a party for consideration. If there is no *prima facie* partisan bias in a recommendation, its promoters may put it forward within *both* parties for adoption.

Many policy initiatives are initially divisive, for example, the Labour Party policy for abolishing grammar schools, or Conservative Party policies on industrial relations legislation. By putting an issue on the agenda for debate the opposition can bring a policy forward for public consideration—but by making it partisan, it can also delay adoption until the party next becomes government. Some initiatives, such as the British application to join the Common Market, can be taken by each party in turn. A Conservative government put forward an application in 1961; Labour reinstated the application in 1966; and a Conservative government applied again in 1970, this time successfully.

Taking an initiative is often the most important thing a party does to influence government policy. By breaking the ring of silence that surrounds a policy, it is effectively "de-routinized." Ministers and shadow ministers are questioned about the desirability of continuing to do what had been taken for granted. The need to justify freshly an existing policy may lead to complete satisfaction, or to second thoughts. If the opposition—or a section of the governing party—is not satisfied with the answers given, it can press for change. The demand for change does not guarantee change—but it is a necessary first step in amending a given policy or introducing a new one in its stead.

A party can create movement on a given issue, but it cannot ensure the direction it will lead. Just as defenders of the status quo may find it difficult to defend their position without adapting it, so too proponents of change face the need to modify their demands. Modifications are necessary to secure the agreement of diverse interests within a party. They will also be important in securing support, or at least grudging acceptance, by affected pressure groups. Finally, a governing party will also need to make changes to meet the weaknesses spotted by civil service advisers and parliamentary draftsmen responsible for turning a statement of intent into a bill to present to Parliament.

When the governing party does present a bill in Parliament, the opposition can adopt one of three alternatives. It can give tacit approval to the measure, not voting against it on second or third reading. The bill then immediately becomes part of the Consensus of British government. Alternatively, it can vote against the bill, as the Adversary model posits—but the bill will still become law. A third alternative, popular among politicians but much neglected in writings about party politics, is to "fudge" an issue. A classic example was given when the Attlee government took the initiative of introducing a National Health Service bill. The Conservative opposition was put on the spot. It would not itself have introduced so ambitious a programme, and its leaders had reservations about the particular proposal put forward. But it did not wish to fight the next election as a party that had voted against a plan providing health care for everyone. Hence, the Conservatives moved reasoned amendments against the bill on second and third readings but did not vote against it in principle. The Conservative spokesman on health fudged the party's position by declaring:

> When we say we wish the bill well we mean that we hope the comprehensive health service to which we are pledged as much as the party opposite will not be retarded or frustrated by what we regard as the vices of this bill.[10]

Enactment fundamentally changes the status of a policy. It is no longer a party's intention but an accomplished fact, a law of the land that any government is expected to uphold, or if it wishes to reverse it, this must be done publicly, with the consequent risk of stimulating Adversary criticism. Once a bill becomes a law, the opposition usually gives it tacit consent, that is, it remains silent. By remaining silent, it does nothing to prevent law-abiding Englishmen from complying with its provisions. Moreover, by being silent, it can avoid being identified as a critic of a measure that may prove to be popular. Interest groups formerly opposed to the bill usually go further. They normally accept a measure as a *fait accompli*, and try to negotiate favourable interpretations of provisions that specially affect their interests.

The government of the day finds that implementing a policy usually makes for a broader consensus. Insofar as it confers benefits upon a group, it creates a new vested interest in favour of the legislation. In order to secure the cooperation of affected interests who cannot be coerced by a parliamentary Whip, the government may have to make significant alterations in administration or even amend the legislation to reduce the potential for criticizing it. The object of the department is to implement it in such a way that it becomes part of the administrative routine. What was once a "moving" element in the policy process becomes part of the stable consensus of unchallenged Acts of Parliament.

If a new policy has been initially opposed by the opposition, it is subject to the final test of consensus when the opposition party is returned to office. It must then administer a law it had once voted against or repeal it. In the great majority of cases, the former adversary of an Act accepts it. A measure that had once divided the parties is added to the thousands of Acts of Parliament that, whatever their origin, are now part of the political consensus.

By definition, there cannot be consensus on all matters; to achieve perfect consensus would mark the end of politics. In the present circumstances of British party politics, there *could* be greater differences between the parties. But if so, what sort of differences would there be?

Judging by the 1979 general election vote, there are clear limits to the demand for change in Britain. The biggest (*sic*) vote for radical change in England[11] went to the National Front, but it polled only 191,706 votes of a total of 31,221,361 cast. At the other end of the political spectrum, the Communist Party polled 16,858 votes, and the Workers' Revolutionary Party, 12,631 votes. An opposition party would not have to go to such extremes to forfeit its prospects for regaining office. Because it is in opposition, any loss of votes is almost certain to doom it to continued political impotence.

One possible consequence of widening the distance between the Conservative and Labour parties is that the electoral pendulum might stop swinging. Since 1945, the average length of time that one party has remained in office has been seven years. But the opposition does not have a guaranteed right to gain office by default of the governing party every half-dozen years or less. If an opposition went to an extreme, it could lose even more popularity than an increasingly accident-prone government party. If both major parties became increasingly unpopular, the Liberals and Nationalists would be at the ready, hoping to prosper.

The disruption of one of the major parties is a second possible consequence of a widening gap between their policies. Any major move to the left in the Labour Party or to the right in the Conservative Party will disturb the so-called centrists within the party, on grounds of both principle and electoral tactics. In the 1979 Parliament, the pressures for change—and therefore, for splitting—are greatest within Labour's ranks. In the 1974 Parliament, the idea of a government of national unity was advanced by supporters of Edward Heath. For decades the Liberals have been waiting for either major party to split, so that they might prosper electorally by alignment with the "centrist" faction in the split.

It is in the prudential interest of each of the major parties not to carry its differences with opponents to the point that it loses significant electoral support or results in a split in the party. This inhibition does not mean that greater differences could not occur in the record of successive Conservative and Labour governments. They are simply a reminder of what can happen to a party that goes too far.

If those party politicians who advocate a greater degree of Adversary competition sustained their case, the net result would not simply be a great swing to the left or to the right. Instead, party government in Britain would be characterized by an abrupt oscillation in public policy, with the direction of government swinging from well on the right to well on the left *and back again* in the course of a decade.[12]

If the alternation of parties in office produced much bigger differences than today, the legal position of trade unions would be fundamentally affected every five years. No council house tenant or mortgage holder could calculate the cost of housing from one Parliament to the next, for it would be altered dramatically with each swing of the electoral pendulum. Prospective pensioners would be faced with new provisions for their old age every time government changed hands at Westminster, and millions of public sector employees would be uncertain of their jobs. Major industries would be nationalized or denationalized in the midst of investment programmes. Nor is this all. No sooner had a local authority digested one reorganization scheme than its boundaries, powers and personnel would once more be thrown in the melting pot to meet the wishes of a newly elected government. Homosexuals could practice free from the fear of legal prosecution only as long as Parliament was dominated by the correct party. Whether a woman could have an abortion or a convicted murderer be hanged might depend upon the timing of a general election. If the parties succeeded in leaving distinctive imprints on the economy, if only by choosing different horns of a dilemma, then unemployment might double and inflation halve under one government, and inflation rates double and unemployment halve under another.

The rapid oscillation of public policy is not what committed partisans have in mind when they advocate greater differences between the parties. They usually assume a "great and irreversible change." But a change can be irreversible only under very limiting and special circumstances. A governing party must have at hand a more powerful social engineering technology than contemporary economics. Insofar as Britain's problems are diagnosed as arising from the "wrong" attitudes of trade unionists or businessmen, then a governing party would require the force of a Stalin, rather than the eloquence of a Keir Hardie or a Winston Churchill, to compel great changes in a short time. Twentieth-century history suggests that great changes in public policy are as likely to arise by accident or as a byproduct of other events as they are to arise from the intent of political parties, for example, the great and rapid changes in Britain in this century forced through by the exigencies and accidents of two world wars.

Models of governing are not to be valued in the abstract. They should be endorsed on the basis of what they do and do not produce. Confronted with the prospect of major policies changing *against* as well as in their favour, and reversing *again and again* with each swing of the electoral pendulum, most active partisans, and certainly the great bulk of the electorate, would say: This is too much. The changes would seem "too much" because they would so greatly increase the uncertainties of life, threatening abrupt reversals in society with every general election—to no particular public purpose. If a referendum could be held, the great bulk of the electorate would almost certainly wish to have fewer and less rapid changes occur in the lifetime of a Parliament, and those that did occur being made secure by a Moving Consensus.

Change endorsed by a Moving Consensus has been the hallmark of British politics for generations. The foundations of the mixed-economy welfare state were laid by interparty discussions and agreement during the Coalition government of 1940–45. Legislation adopted by the 1945–51 Attlee government was often criticized by the Conservatives, but few measures were actually repealed thereafter. Up to 1979, each of the two major parties had been in power for seventeen years since the end of the Second World War, and each had accepted the great bulk of the legislation enacted by its opponents.

Ironically, in the 1979 general election campaign it was the Labour Party rather than the nominally Conservative Party that vociferously urged maintaining a Moving Consensus in government. Labour warned against the risk of change, and once Mrs. Thatcher had won, James Callaghan warned of the dire consequences of radical change. Echoing arguments that Winston Churchill had used to attack the policies of the 1945–51 Labour government, Callaghan alleged:

> What is happening today is much more than the normal change of policies that a country expects when a new government is elected. What we are seeing today is an attempt to take us back to the nineteenth century.[14]

Mrs. Thatcher, as was her privilege, talked of giving the electorate a chance to vote for a major change in the way Britain is governed. As she explained to the 1979 Conservative Party Conference:

> Those who voted Conservative know the principles we stand for. We have every right to carry them out and we shall.[15]

Into the 1980s

Judged by past performance, the constraints upon any British government, Conservative or Labour, are stronger than ideological intentions. On the most important issue facing the country, the management of the economy, both parties would like to make a break from their immediate past. Instead of continuing to manage a negative trend in many major economic indicators, each party would like to preside over a reversal of trends. Any party that produced a rate of economic growth above the European average, increased both take-home pay and the benefits of public policy without difficulty, and reduced inflation and unemployment, would make a welcome difference from the governments of Britain in the 1970s.

Immediately, the Conservatives must take responsibility for governing the country, and the government of Margaret Thatcher clearly wishes to make a difference to the country. Given the drift of national events previously, the question one must ask is: How much difference can the Conservatives hope to make to the country between 1979 and 1984? The answer to this question depends upon what is perceived as "do-able" by the purposeful action of British government today. The

Conservatives undoubtedly have the parliamentary right to attempt what they will, but it is far from clear whether they have the power to achieve what they will.

In the first Queen's Speech to Parliament on 15 May 1979, the new Conservative government brought forward a number of proposals that could result in Adversary divisions in the House of Commons: legislation on industrial relations; changes in the 1975 Industry Act and the Labour-created National Enterprise Board, and in the scope for private health care; and selective and fee-paying education. In the budget of 12 June 1979, the government introduced further controversial measures, increasing the value-added tax to 15 percent, and cutting income tax specially on the top ranges. Yet many of the measures in the Queen's Speech of the the Conservative government could be endorsed by any party — a wish for peace in the Middle East, a desire to safeguard historic buildings and artistic treasures and a revision of Britain's contribution to the finances of the European Economic Community.

No sooner had the Conservatives launched their "new departure" budget than publicly and privately speculation commenced about how long the government would continue in this direction, and how soon it would be for the first signs of a U-turn in policy to appear. As *The Economist* put it:

> Like *tricoteuses*, Treasury-watchers sit round a new government waiting for the slaughter of proudly proclaimed economic policies. Place your bets now for which Tory principle gets the chop in Sir Geoffrey Howe's 1980 budget.[16]

The analysis leading to such a conclusion is not based on party spite, or the dismissal of politicians as deceptive by nature, for any U-turn would be a sign that politicians were first of all deceiving themselves. Instead, it is derived from appreciation of the dilemmas that face any government trying to attain a wide variety of not always compatible economic objectives. Good intentions and a strong will are not enough to produce an improvement in the British economy if the secular trends and constraints chronicled here remain as strong in the next five years as in the past twenty years.

The less economics one knows, the easier it is to spot the political pressure that would most likely lead the Conservative government (or any government) to rethink its economic policies: by-election defeats. In the abstract, the Conservative majority is large enough to be proof against any normal number of by-election setbacks. But the party's morale would have to be abnormally strong to avoid questioning policies and personalities if Labour or Liberal MPs began to occupy seats that until then were thought safely in Conservative hands.

In opposition, Labour is free from the constraints as well as the perquisites of office. But Labour's dominance of government from 1964 to 1979 and James Callaghan's personal identification with that record launched the opposition into a new Parliament defending Labour's past record, but doing so without the resources available in office.

The immediate problems of the Labour leadership are internal to the party. They are both ideological and organizational. Ideologically, the leadership is vulnerable to the left-wing charge that its policies and intentions, roughly described by the label Social Democracy, have been tried and failed.[17] The Labour leadership cannot deny that it was responsible for the nation's economy for most of the past fifteen years. It cannot claim that its policies were approved by such left-wing weeklies as *Tribune* or *Militant*, nor would it wish to claim that they were Tory. To argue that Labour governments coped as well as could be expected in the face of unfavourable secular trends is to invite the retort that a Socialist government should create such economic discontinuities that the negative trends of the mixed economy would no longer be a worry. (Critics would suggest that other and worse problems would arise instead.) Articulate Social Democrats appear to accept much of the criticism of the record of Labour government. Rather than look to the past for confidence and inspiration, they speak of the need for a new guide for action to replace Anthony Crosland's *The Future of Socialism*, published in 1956.[18]

Left-wing critics of the Labour government's record combined an ideological and organizational initiative to win a sweeping victory for a programme to change the power structure of the Labour Party at its 1979 Annual Conference at Brighton. In opposition, the party's National Executive Committee may claim to be the chief spokesmen for "the movement." Whereas Labour Cabinets and the Parliamentary Committee elected in the 1979–80 session of Parliament tend to be moderate, the NEC is currently left-dominated, and distant from a ministerialist outlook. The Conference elected only three ex-Cabinet Ministers to the NEC—Anthony Benn, Judith Hart and Shirley Williams—and rejected five ex-ministers. The Labour Party's next election manifesto may mark a radical break with the Moving Consensus of the past. Nonetheless, it will still be haunted by the perennial question: Why has every Labour government since the first in 1924 governed as part of a Moving Consensus rather than as a radical Adversary?

While the outcome of the debate within the Labour Party is unclear at the time of writing, one point immediately stands out: either the party leader, James Callaghan, or the 1979 party chairman, Frank Allaun, is completely wrong in his estimate of the scope for policy differences between a Conservative and a Labour government. If the parliamentary leadership is fortunate, it may be gifted victory at the next election by Mrs. Thatcher's government widening the gap between the parties in a way that the bulk of the electorate finds unsatisfactory. Alternatively, the Labour Party may, by moving left, so widen the gap that it fails to gain electoral support, whatever the difficulties of the Conservative government. Given that at the 1979 general election Labour won only 36.9 percent of the vote, its lowest since 1931, it has no margin of safety should it miscalculate the effect of new policies on the electorate.

In a free society, any political party has the right to be as different as it wishes from its political opponents. But it cannot expect to win a general election if it chooses to be "too" different. The price it pays is not only its own exclusion from office but the confirmation in office of its distrusted Adversary.

Twice in the past two decades, American political parties have decided to offer the American electorate "a choice, not an echo." In 1964 Republicans dissatisfied with what they saw as the "me too" policies of moderate Republican candidates nominated Barry Goldwater for the Presidency with Milton Friedman among his advisers. Goldwater received 38.5 percent of the vote, slightly less than Herbert Hoover polled when defeated by Franklin D. Roosevelt in 1932. Eight years later, reacting against internal party dissatisfaction with the last years of the Johnson Presidency, Democrats nominated George McGovern as their standard bearer. Running from the opposite end of the political spectrum, McGovern polled an even smaller share of the vote, 37.5 percent, than Goldwater, and gifted Richard Nixon an even bigger margin of victory than Johnson had gained in 1964. The scale of defeat made the parties think again. In each case, by reversing its course and moving to the political centre, the party went from a landslide defeat to victory at the next presidential election.

The British election due by 1984 will not mark an Orwellian end of time. It will be but one more step in the endless journey of representative government. The party that wins control of the next Parliament will differ in some of its intentions and policies from its opponents. But the differences in practice may be less than some voters (and some MPs) expect. Moreover, in the management of the economy changes may be less (or different) than many voters would wish. Neither the Labour nor the Conservative Party can expect to make all the difference to British society by winning a general election.

Britain has a long tradition of party government, but it does not have a tradition of the totalitarian party state, which admits no constraints upon government. Faced with a choice between a government with too much or too little power, the British tradition is to make the first charge upon government maintaining political consent.

Notes

Introduction

1. See, e.g., A. H. Birch, *Representative and Responsible Government* (London: Allen & Unwin, 1964), pp. 243 ff; R. T. McKenzie, *British Political Parties* (2nd ed.; London: Heinemann, 1963), chap. 11; and Samuel H. Beer, *Modern British Politics* (London: Faber & Faber, 1965).

2. Cf. D. E. Butler and Dennis Kavanagh, *The British General Election of February, 1974* (London: Macmillan, 1974), pp. 10 and 50.

3. *The Economist*, 5 November 1977. See also S. E. Finer's editorial introduction to *Adversary Politics and Electoral Reform* (London: Clive Wigram, 1975), pp. 12 ff.

4. Lord Hailsham, *The Dilemma of Democracy* (London: Collins, 1978).

5. Roy Jenkins, "Home Thoughts from Abroad," *The Listener*, 29 November 1979.

6. Ibid.

7. This and subsequent manifesto quotes are taken from the complete texts in *The Times Guide to the House of Commons, May, 1979* (London: Times Books, 1979), pp. 282–323.

8. "Why Labour voters should take a chance on Mrs. T," *Sunday Telegraph*, 29 April 1979.

9. Lord McCarthy, "The Politics of Incomes Policy," in *Policy and Politics: Essays in Honour of Norman Chester*, ed. David Butler and A. H. Halsey (London: Macmillan, 1978), p. 183.

Chapter 1. *Parties and Public Policy*

1. See Richard Rose, *What is Governing? Purpose and Policy in Washington* (Englewood Cliffs, N.J.; Prentice-Hall, 1978), pp. 13 f.

2. The section thus supplements and expands conditions set out in Richard Rose, *The Problem of Party Government* (London: Macmillan, 1974), pp. 380 ff.

3. For the author's reply to this question, see Richard Rose, *Politics in England* (3rd ed.; London: Faber & Faber, 1980), chap. 10.

4. See, e.g., Leon D. Epstein, *Political Parties in Western Democracies* (New York: Praeger, 1967), and Evron M. Kirkpatrick, "Toward a More Responsible Two-Party System: Political Science, Policy Science or Pseudo-Science?" *American Political Science Review* 65, no. 4 (1971), a critique of "Toward a More Responsible Two-Party System: a Report of the Committee on Political Parties, American Political Science Association," ibid., 44, no. 3 (1950), Supplement.

5. Robert T. McKenzie, *British Political Parties* (London: Heinemann, 1963 ed.) p. vi.

6. Ralph Miliband, *Parliamentary Socialism* (London: Allen & Unwin, 1967).

7. Contrast the views of Samuel H. Beer, *Modern British Politics* (London: Faber & Faber, 1965), with Otto Kirchheimer, "The Transformation of the Western European Party Systems" in *Political Parties and Political Development*, ed. Joseph LaPalombara

and Myron Weiner (Princeton: Princeton University Press, 1966), and S. M. Lipset, "The Changing Class Structure and Contemporary European Politics," *Daedalus* 93, no. 1 (1964): 271 ff.

8. See Rose, *The Problem of Party Government*, chap. 12.

9. Cf. Lewis Minkin, *The Labour Party Conference* (London: Allen Lane, 1978), and McKenzie, *British Political Parties*.

10. "Spatial Models of Party Competition," in Angus Campbell, Philip E. Converse, Warren E. Miller and Donald E. Stokes, *Elections and the Political Order* (New York: Wiley, 1966), p. 170.

11. Quintin Hogg (intermittently, Lord Hailsham), *The Conservative Case* (Harmondsworth: Penguin, 1959), p. 16. For a classic description of this process, see Anthony Downs, *An Economic Theory of Democracy* (New York: Harper & Row, 1957).

12. See Giovanni Sartori, "European Political Parties: the Case of Polarized Pluralism," in LaPalombara and Weiner, *Political Parties and Political Development*, pp. 137 ff.

13. Richard Rose, *Northern Ireland: A Time of Choice* (London: Macmillan, 1976).

14. See William B. Gwyn and Richard Rose, eds., *Britain—Progress and Decline* (London: Macmillan, 1980).

Chapter 2. *Adversary or Consensus Politics?*

1. Bernard Crick, *The Reform of Parliament* (2nd ed.; London: Weidenfeld & Nicolson, 1964), p. 245. Italics in the original.

2. See R. M. Punnett, *Front-Bench Opposition* (London: Heinemann, 1973), chap. 6.

3. Quoted in D. E. Butler and Richard Rose, *The British General Election of 1959* (London: Macmillan, 1960), pp. 32–33.

4. "Introduction" to Walter Bagehot, *The English Constitution* (London: World's Classics ed., 1955), p. xxiv.

5. For a discussion of the specific content of cultural consensus in England, see Richard Rose, *Politics in England* (3rd ed.; London: Faber & Faber, 1980), chap. 4.

6. See D. E. Butler and Dennis Kavanagh, *The British General Election of October, 1974* (London: Macmillan, 1975), pp. 286 f. See also pp. 43–50, 122 ff.

7. See Peter Kellner, "Coalition," *Sunday Times*, 14 May 1978. The idea is not new. See R. Bassett, *The Essentials of Parliamentary Democracy* (London: Macmillan, 1935);and David Butler, ed., *Coalitions in British Politics* (London: Macmillan, 1978).

8. Godfrey Barker, "Mrs. Thatcher's Team 6: Lord Carrington," *Daily Telegraph*, 15 July 1978.

9. McKenzie, *British Political Parties*, p. 646.

10. Joseph A. Schumpeter, *Capitalism, Socialism and Democracy* (4th ed.; London: Allen & Unwin, 1952), p. 291.

11. See D. E. Butler, "The Paradox of Party Difference," in *Studies in British Politics*, ed. Richard Rose (3rd ed.; London: Macmillan, 1976).

12. See Richard Rose, "The Political Ideas of English Party Activists," *American Political Science Review* 56, no. 2 (1962).

13. See Harold J. Laski, *Parliamentary Government in England* (London: Allen & Unwin, 1938), pp. 93, 63.

14. For Laski's recantation, see his *Reflections on the Constitution* (Manchester: University Press, 1951).

15. A prior assumption of this model is that the manifestos of the two parties are not identical. This is in fact the case. See chapter 5 *infra*.

16. Michael Oakeshott, *Political Education* (Cambridge: Bowes & Bowes, 1951), p. 11.

17. *The English Constitution*, p. 128.
18. See D. E. Butler and Anthony S. King, *The British General Election of 1966* (London: Macmillan, 1966), p. 5.
19. See *The Economist*, 13 February 1954, p. 440.
20. See Richard Rose, "Disciplined Research and Undisciplined Problems," *International Social Science Journal* 28, no. 1 (1976): 105 ff.
21. Up to the late 1960s, Labour was often regarded as normally displaying an opposition mentality, and the Conservatives, a government mentality. But such generalizations are hardly applicable to a Labour parliamentary frontbench after eleven years in office from 1964, whatever their relevance to their opponents in the extraparliamentary Labour Party. Nor can Conservative leaders be regarded as "natural" governors when, like Edward Heath and Margaret Thatcher, they serve first in the wilderness of opposition, and have relatively humble social origins.

Chapter 3. *The Choice at Elections*

1. See Richard Rose, "Britain: Simple Abstractions and Complex Realities," in *Electoral Behavior: A Comparative Handbook*, ed. R. Rose (New York: Free Press, 1974). Very similar statistical evidence is presented in David Butler and Donald Stokes, *Political Change in Britain* (2nd ed.; London: Macmillan, 1974), but their interpretation differs, as they tend to regard any deviation from an absolutely random pattern of voting as evidence of class divisions.
2. See Rose, "Britain: Simple Abstractions and Complex Realities," p. 510.
3. The results of AID analysis of elections from 1959 through 1970 can be found in Richard Rose, *The Problem of Party Government* (London: Macmillan, 1974), pp. 494–97. The author's analysis of subsequent Gallup surveys shows that the proportion of the Conservative-Labour division of the vote explained by standard socioeconomic influences was 17.6 percent in February 1974; 18.7 percent in October 1974; and 12.3 percent in 1979.
4. The proportion of variance explained is low because, given two classes and two parties, upwards of half the voters might randomly vote for their class-typical party, and the statistical algorithm discounts random relationships.
5. The mean of the Conservative-Labour share of the vote explained in seven elections, 1959–79, is 17.8 percent. When this is taken as a proportion of the total electorate, the mean falls to 11.6 percent.
6. See Richard Rose, "Introduction," in Rose, ed., *Electoral Behavior*, p. 17. In many lands, including Northern Ireland, religion is the chief influence on voting—and stronger than class in Britain.
7. The figures reported in table 3.2 underestimate the proportion of electors not voting in 1979, since surveys normally overrepresent voters. If nonvoters were in their true proportion, the extent of class-typical voting would be reduced to about 38 percent. But this would be misleading, inasmuch as many nonvoters are not persistent abstainers, and align with the major parties on a similar basis as voters. Cf. Ivor Crewe, Tony Fox and Jim Alt, "Non-Voting in British General Elections, 1966–October 1974," in *British Political Sociology Yearbook*, ed. Colin Crouch (London: Croom-Helm, 1977), vol. 3.
8. For a review of the variety of motives in Conservative voting, see Dennis A. Kavanagh, "The Deferential English: A Comparative Critique," in *Government and Opposition* 6, no. 3 (1971).
9. *Gallup Political Index*, no. 225 (May 1979): 21.
10. For results of similar analyses coming to similar conclusion, earlier in the 1970s, see Rose, *The Problem of Party Government*, p. 308; Richard Rose, *Politics in England*

(3rd ed.; London: Faber & Faber, 1980), table 12.1; and Richard Rose, "Resistance to Moral Change," *New Society*, 12 April 1979.

11. *Gallup Political Index*, no. 203 (May 1977): 10.

12. See David Robertson, *A Theory of Party Competition* (London: Wiley, 1976), p. 80. This factor accounts for 26.8 percent of the total variance.

13. The convergence towards consensus is even more striking on the second factor identified by Robertson, ibid., p. 101, accounting for an additional 19.4 percent of the total variance.

14. See Monica Charlot, *La Démocratie L'Anglaise* (Paris: Armand Colin, 1972) chap. 6. The classification scheme is that originally developed by Kenneth Janda of Northwestern University for the systematic international comparison of political parties. For additional confirmation, see John Clayton Thomas, "The Changing Nature of Partisan Divisions in the West," *European Journal of Political Research* 7, no. 4 (1979): 397–413.

15. Derived from ibid., p. 212.

16. See David Robertson, "The Content of Election Addresses and Leaders' Speeches," in *The British General Election of 1970*, ed. D. E. Butler and Michael Pinto-Duschinsky (London: Macmillan, 1971), p. 441 f.

17. See D. E. Butler and Dennis Kavanagh, *The British General Election of 1979* (London: Macmillan, 1980), chap. 15.

18. Shelley Pinto-Duschinsky, "A Matter of Words," *New Society*, 7 March 1974.

19. Michael Pinto-Duschinsky, "False Calm: Party Strategies in October, 1974," in *Britain at the Polls: the Parliamentary Elections of 1974*, ed. Howard Penniman (Washington, D.C.: American Enterprise Institute, 1975), p. 203.

Chapter 4. *Testing the Manifesto*

1. Wilfrid Harrison, *The Government of Britain* (5th ed.; London: Hutchinson, 1958), p. 164.

2. For the evolution of practices that led to the modern manifesto, see Cecil S. Emden, *The People and the Constitution* (Oxford: Clarendon Press, 1933), esp. chap. 1.

3. See F. W. S. Craig, *British General Election Manifestos, 1900–1974* (London: Macmillan, 1975), pp. 2 ff.

4. S. E. Finer, "Manifesto Moonshine," *New Society*, 13 November 1975.

5. Ibid.

6. Anthony S. King, "Death of the Manifesto," *The Observer*, 17 February 1974. King's views are echoed by Sidney Weighell, an NUR member of the Labour Party Enquiry, 1980, in "What Labour Must Do to Avoid Another Defeat," *The Times*, 28 December 1979.

7. Geoff Bish, Secretary of the Research Department of the Labour Party, "Working Relations between Government and Party," in *What Went Wrong*, ed. Ken Coates (Nottingham: Spokesman for Institute for Workers' Control, 1979), p. 163.

8. In October 1974, 73 percent of Conservative and 62 percent of Labour candidates said they paid a "great deal" of attention to their party manifesto, and less than one-tenth said they gave it little or no attention. See D. E. Butler and Dennis Kavanagh, *The British General Election of October, 1974* (London: Macmillan, 1975), p. 230.

9. King, "Death of the Manifesto."

10. "Tory Policy 'Not influenced by Decisions,'" *Daily Telegraph*, 21 September 1978.

11. See J. D. Hoffman, *The Conservative Party in Opposition, 1945–51* (London: MacGibbon & Kee, 1964); Harold Macmilllan, *Memoirs*, vol. 5, *Pointing the Way, 1959–61* (London: Macmillan, 1972), pp. 4–5, and Chris Patten, "Policy Making in Op-

position," in *Conservative Party Politics*, ed. Zig Layton-Henry (London: Macmillan, 1980), pp. 9–24, and other contributions to that volume.

12. Conservative Research Department, *Politics Today*, no. 15 (8 October 1979): 315–18.

13. For an exhaustive study of extraparliamentary Labour policy making in this period, see Lewis Minkin, *The Labour Party Conference* (London: Allen Lane, 1978).

14. The words of George Brown, *In My Way* (Harmondsworth: Penguin, 1972), pp. 252 f.

15. Quoted in Minkin, *The Labour Party Conference*, p. 312.

16. See pp. 6–7 of *Labour's Programme 1976* (London: Labour Party) for some positive-sounding but ultimately inconclusive phrases by the party's General Secretary, whose Foreword had the unenviable task of trying to emphasize the importance of the intentions announced therein by the extraparliamentary party without immediately upsetting the Labour government.

17. Geoff Bish, "Drafting the Manifesto," in Coates, *What Went Wrong*, p. 189. Cf. Michael Hatfield, *The House the Left Built* (London: Victor Gollancz, 1978).

18. Bish, "Drafting the Manifesto," p. 190. Italics added.

19. Geoff Bish, "Working Relations between Government and Party," p. 164.

20. See R. H. S. Crossman, *Inside View* (London: Jonathan Cape, 1972).

21. Initially, it was intended to analyze the 1964–70 Labour government's record, but this proved impracticable, because of the complications introduced by Labour's very small majority over the Conservatives in the first two sessions, when the manifesto might normally be strongest, and the interruption caused by the 1966 general election. The record of that period generally confirms evidence presented here for the 1974–79 Labour government.

22. See "Labour's Record," *Labour Weekly*, 6 April 1979; and *The Campaign Guide 1974* (London: Conservative Central Office, 1974), pp. 684–95.

23. See, e.g., *The Campaign Guide 1974*, p. 685; and the statement by Fred Corfield, *House of Commons Debates*, vol. 810, col. 1922–35 (4 February 1971).

24. In 1970, the parties joined issue with each other on 22 of 155 policies, and in 1974 on 28 of 204 issues.

25. Kenneth Harris, *The Prime Minister talks to The Observer* (London: The Observer, 1979), p. 11.

26. An examination of the opposition's use of Supply Days shows that manifesto pledges are not a primary cause of Adversary divisions there. Opposition criticism in Supply Days tends to be very general or focuses on immediate, tactical shortcomings and difficulties of the government. The opposition is not anxious to repeat manifesto pledges from an election that it lost. Cf. table 5.5.

Chapter 5. *Adversary Parliament and Consensus Legislation*

1. On the complexity of relations between these interest groups and government, see, e.g., Gerald A. Dorfman, *Government versus Trade Unionism in British Politics since 1968* (London: Macmillan, 1979); and Wyn Grant and David Marsh, *The Confederation of British Industry* (London: Hodder & Stoughton, 1977).

2. For a discussion of the free votes analyzed here, see Peter G. Richards, *Parliament and Conscience* (London: Allen & Unwin, 1970); the figures are conveniently given in Richard Rose, *The Problem of Party Government* (London: Macmillan, 1974), table 11.3.

3. "Policy Differences in British Parliamentary Parties," *American Political Science Review* 65, no. 3 (1971). Data from p. 698 as summarized in Rose, *The Problem of Party Government*, table 11.3.

4. See Robert D. Putnam, *The Beliefs of Politicians* (New Haven: Yale University Press, 1973), figure 4.2.

5. Norman Wilding and Philip Laundy, *An Encyclopedia of Parliament* (London: Cassel & Co., 1961 ed.), p. 378.

6. Extending the analysis to include the 1968/69 and 1969/70 sessions of the Commons, utilizing earlier Ivor Burton and Gavin Drewry research reported in *Parliamentary Affairs* 23, no. 2 (1970): 154–83, and 13, no. 4 (1970): 308–44, confirms the conclusions drawn from evidence of the 1970s.

7. In the 1974–79 Parliament, the Conservative-dominated House of Lords was often out of sympathy with the Labour government, but the proportion of bills divided against actually dropped to six percent to avoid frequent defeats for the Labour government.

8. See Ivor Burton and Gavin Drewry, "Public Legislation: A Survey of the Session 1968/69," *Parliamentary Affairs* 23, no. 2 (1970): 161 f.

9. Philip Norton, *Conservative Dissidents* (London: Temple Smith, 1978), and *Dissension in the House of Commons 1974–79* (London: Oxford University Press, forthcoming), provide detailed case studies complementing his comprehensive mapping, reported in *Dissension in the House of Commons* (London: Macmillan, 1975).

10. House of Commons *Debates* vol. 854, col. 951 (9 April 1973).

11. House of Commons *Debates* vol. 911, col. 1237 (18 May 1976).

12. In the final two sessions of the 1966–70 Parliament, the Conservatives divided against the Labour government more often (67 percent of 42 motions), but this was still substantially less than Labour's rate in the 1970–74 Parliament.

13. Divisions can, of course, be called by Liberals, Nationalist, Ulster or dissident MPs. But without the support of the Official Opposition, such divisions only advertise the weakness of third parties.

14. It is also possible to reverse measures by administrative acts. This is specially important in the management of the economy. But see chap. 7.

15. Calculated from data in *Parliamentary Affairs* articles by Ivor Burton and Gavin Drewry, "Public Legislation 1969–70" (vol. 23, no. 4, 1970); 1970–71 (vol. 25, no. 2, 1972); 1974 (vol. 29, no. 2, 1976); 1974–75 (vol. 30, no. 2, 1977).

16. Ivor Burton and Gavin Drewry, "Public Legislation in 1973/74 and a Parliament in Retrospect," *Parliamentary Affairs* 28, no. 2 (1975): 141.

Chapter 6. *Reorganizing Government: Partisanship without Technocracy*

1. E. E. Schattschneider, *The Semi-Sovereign People* (New York: Holt, Rinehart & Winston, 1960), p. 71. Italics in the original.

2. For a review of the mood of the period, see William B. Gwyn and Richard Rose, eds., *Britain—Progress and Decline* (London: Macmillan, 1980); for an institutional review, see, e. g., W. Thornhill, ed., *The Modernization of British Government* (London: Pitman, 1975).

3. See D. E. Butler, *The Electoral System in Britain since 1918* (2nd ed.; Oxford: Clarendon Press, 1963), chap. 5.

4. See D. E. Butler, "The Redistribution of Seats," *Public Administration* 32, no. 2 (1955): 140.

5. See House of Commons, *Debates*, vol. 791, esp. col. 428 (12 November 1969), and vol. 774, col. 436 (26 November 1968).

6. Cmnd. 6601 (London: HMSO, 1976).

7. David Butler, "Modifying Electoral Arrangements," in *Policy and Politics,* ed. D. E. Butler and A. H. Halsey (London: Macmillan, 1978), p. 17.

8. See Richard Rose, *Northern Ireland: Time of Choice* (London: Macmilllan, 1976).

9. For a "good government" view, see the *Report of the Royal Commission on the Constitution* (London: HMSO, Cmnd. 5460, 1973). For a political science analysis, see Vernon Bogdanor, *Devolution* (London: Oxford University Press, 1979).

10. For relevant documents, see Cmnd. 4040 (1969), Cmnd. 4276 (1970) and Cmnd. 4584 (1971). For a review of the problems and literature, see Ken Young, "Environmental Management in Local Politics," in *New Trends in British Politics*, ed. Dennis Kavanagh and Richard Rose (London: Sage Publications, 1976).

11. Bernard Crick, *The Reform of Parliament* (London: Weidenfeld & Nicolson, 1964), p. ix. For the views of MPs, see Appendix B of Crick's volume and Anthony Barker and Michael Rush, *The Member of Parliament and His Information* (London: Allen & Unwin, 1970).

12. S. A. Walkland, "Whither the Commons?" in *The Commons in the 70s*, ed. S. A. Walkland and Michael Ryle (London: Fontana, 1977), p. 243. Cf. the guarded optimism of the previous study by the same group, A. H. Hanson and Bernard Crick, eds., *The Commons in Transition* (London: Fontana, 1970).

13. Sir Richard Clarke, "The Machinery of Government," in Thornhill, *The Modernization of British Government*, p. 81.

14. *The Civil Service* (London: HMSO, Cmnd. 3638, 1968), vol. 1, para. 14.

15. Ibid., p. 181.

16. See House of Commons, *Debates*, 21 November 1968, vol. 773, cols. 1542–60.

17. L. J. Sharpe, "Whitehall—Structures and People," in Kavanagh and Rose, eds., *New Trends in British Politics*, p. 58.

18. See *The Civil Service*, vol. 1, pp. 27 ff and Appendix E, esp. p. 162.

19. Gerald Caiden, writing about America in words equally apt for Britain: "The Current Wave of Administrative Reform in the USA," *Public Administration Bulletin*, no. 30 (August 1979): 4.

Chapter 7. *Managing the Economy: Neither Technocracy nor Ideology*

1. For an elegant statement of the vulnerability of national economies to international influences, see Assar Lindbeck, "Stabilization Policy in Open Economies with Endogenous Politicians," *American Economic Review* 66, no. 2 (1976): 1–19.

2. See S. E. Finer, ed., *Adversary Politics and Electoral Reform* (London: Anthony Wigram, 1975), esp. the contributions by Tom Wilson and D. K. Stout.

3. See Richard Rose and B. Guy Peters, *The Juggernaut of Incrementalism* (Glasgow: University of Strathclyde Studies in Public Policy, no. 24, 1978).

4. See, e.g., W. L. Miller and Myles Mackie, "The Electoral Cycle and the Asymmetry of Government and Opposition Popularity," *Political Studies* 21, no. 3 (1973); and Edward R. Tufte, *Political Control of the Economy* (Princeton: Princeton University Press, 1978).

5. If attention is concentrated on whether the deficit rises or falls, there is again no evidence of consistent partisan difference. Budget deficits rose in five of ten years of Labour government, and eight of eleven years of Conservative government.

6. See Richard Rose and B. Guy Peters, *Can Government Go Bankrupt?* (New York: Basic Books, 1978) pp. 135 ff.

7. On the variety of pressures increasing public spending, see ibid., chap. 5; and for a theoretical critique, see Daniel Tarschys, "The Growth of Public Expenditure: Nine Modes of Explanation," *Scandinavian Political Studies* 10 (Oslo: Universitetsforlaget, 1974).

8. For the sake of consistency, calendar year public expenditure since 1957 is calculated by the old Treasury method, which includes public corporations' capital expendi-

ture, including that from internally generated funds. On the slightly lower new basis, the 1974 ratio of public expenditure to the national product was 53.0 percent, and the 1975 proportion, 55.7 percent.

9. The correlation is 0.931; r^2, 0.867, the B value, 0.771, and significance 0.00. While high, the level of statistical explanation is not quite so high as in figure 7.3 because annual changes in the national product can affect the PE/GDP ratio as well as changes in public expenditure.

10. See *National Income and Expenditure, 1968* (London: HMSO, 1968), table 53; *1974* (London: HMSO, 1975) pp. 131–4; and *Financial Statistics, September 1978* (London: HMSO), p. 151.

11. For a more detailed discussion of changes in programme spending, see Rudolf Klein, "The Politics of Public Expenditure," *British Journal of Political Science* 6, no. 4 (1976).

12. The data reported here are based on new programme entries and nil entries in Public Expenditure White Paper reports of detailed departmental spending categories, Cmnd. 5519 (1973 survey prices) and Cmnd. 7439 (1978 survey prices). A measure of tolerance should be allowed for changes in Treasury programme categories, but this does not alter the general conclusion reported here.

13. For an analysis of overspending and underspending on particular programmes, see Quentin Outram, *The Significance of Public Expenditure Plans* (London: Centre for Studies in Social Policy, 1975).

14. Intended and actual percentage growth in public spending are as follows: Labour government (Wilson): intended 14.8 percent; actual 29.1 percent, 1966/67–1969/70. Conservatives (Heath): intended 6.2 percent; actual 20.2 percent, 1971/72–1973/74. Data from Public Expenditure publications: Cmnd. 2915, p. 24; Cmnd. 4234, p. 15; Cmnd. 5519, table 2A; Cmnd. 4578, table 1; Cmnd. 5519, Table 2A; Cmnd. 5879, Table 3.1; Cmnd. 5879, table 3.1; 1978/79 Cmnd. 7439, table 3, line 7 (estimated outturn, 1978/79).

15. See Maurice Wright, "Public Expenditure in Britain: The Crisis of Control," *Public Administration* 55 (Summer 1977). Wright's article shows the failure of PESC (the Public Expenditure Survey Committee) to provide a technocratically effective means of controlling public expenditure in the face of economic turbulence and unanticipated political exigencies.

16. The fluctuations are so large that there is a weak correlation (– 0.194) between time and annual growth rates, a low r^2, 0.038, and a small B value, – 0.034.

17. See "The Wages of Fear," *New Society* 1 (February 1979): 243–44. The wages depicted in figure 7.6 are figures for October of the year cited; hence, the October 1978 figure is properly interpreted as indicating the state of wages in the run up to the May 1979 general election.

18. The problem is not unique to Britain. Italy and Sweden face it as well. See Rose and Peters, *Can Government Go Bankrupt?*, chap. 7.

19. Of the making of measures of income distribution there is no end. The two measures used here were selected because of their electoral salience and availability for the time period, without prior knowledge of what results they would yield. The broad conclusions would not be altered by the use of other indicators. Even data that showed no change in the distribution of wealth or earnings would equally show a nil secular trend, also rejecting the idea that parties made a difference by altering income distribution. For the most comprehensive data on income distribution, see *Reports* of the Royal Commission on the Distribution of Income and Wealth (London: HMSO, 1975–79).

20. Because the data *appeared* to show the existence of two discrete periods with different levels of unemployment, trend analyses were also run for subperiods, but the trend lines generated did not fit as well as that shown in figure 7.8. For the period 1948–78, the r^2 was 0.598; for 1957–70, 0.206; and for 1971–78, 0.652.

21. See C. A. E. Goodhart and R. J. Bhansali, "Political Economy," *Political Studies* 18, no. 1 (1970). For a later discussion of the same problem, see Paul Mosley, "Images of the Floating Voter; or, the Political Business Cycle Revisited," *Political Studies* 26, no. 3 (1978): 375–94; and Bruno S. Frey and Friedrich Schneider, "A Politico-Economic Model of the United Kingdom," *Economic Journal* 88 (June 1978): 243–53.

22. Douglas Hibbs, "Political Parties and Macroeconomic Policy," *American Political Science Review* 71, no. 4 (1977): 1481, attempts to simulate the partisan effect of what he calculates to be a 0.3 percent change in unemployment under a Conservative or Labour government, rising with the former and falling with the latter. The analysis is invalid in two respects. As figure 7.8 shows, there is an element of cyclical fluctuation within each period of party government. Moreover, Hibbs' failure to utilize data since 1972 – and *especially* since the return of the Labour government in March 1974 – means that the simulation is based upon a period of British economic history very different from that of the past decade.

23. See "The Dons Who Want to Go to Market," *The Observer*, 24 October 1971.

24. C. A. E. Goodhart, "Monetary Policy," in *Demand Management*, ed. Michael Posner (London: Heinemann Educational Books, 1978), p. 188.

25. See, e. g., Wilfred Beckerman, ed., *The Labour Government's Economic Record, 1964–1970* (London: Duckworth, 1972); and Ralph Harris and Brendan Sewill, *British Economic Policy 1970–74; Two Views* (London: Institute of Economic Affairs, 1975).

26. It is said that when Keynes initially voiced this epigram, a quick-witted Cambridge colleague corrected him thus: "No. In the long run, each of us is dead."

Chapter 8. *Something Stronger Than Parties*

1. See Richard Rose, Ian McAllister and Peter Mair, *Is There a Concurring Majority about Northern Ireland?* (Glasgow: University of Strathclyde Studies in Public Policy, no. 22, 1978).

2. See Stein Rokkan, "Votes Count, Resources Decide," in *Makt og Motiv* (Oslo: Gyldendal Norskforlag, 1976).

3. Peter Hennessy, "Mrs. Thatcher warned in secret report of certain defeat in confrontation with Unions," *The Times*, 15 April 1978.

4. For a detailed discussion of intraparty divisions, see Richard Rose, *The Problem of Party Government* (London: Macmillan, 1974), chap. 12.

5. See Ken Coates, ed., *What Went Wrong?* (Nottingham: Spokesman for Institute for Workers' Control, 1979).

6. Walter Bagehot, *The English Constitution* (London: World's Classics ed., 1955), chap. 1.

7. "Mandarin Power," *The Sunday Times*, 10 June 1973. On Richard Crossman's surprise on learning that governments (and ministers) have departments and departmental interests, see Grant Jordan, "Central Coordination, Crossman and the Inner Cabinet," *Political Quarterly* 49, no. 2 (1978).

8. *The Listener*, 29 November 1979.

9. For a fuller development of the process, see Richard Rose, "Comparing Public Policy," *European Journal of Political Research* 1, no. 1 (1973): 75–82.

10. Sir Henry Willink, House of Commons *Debates*, vol. 426, col. 458 (26 July 1946).

11. Nationalist parties in Scotland and Wales, and almost all parties in Northern Ireland, are extremist by English standards. Alternatively, it could be argued that exposure to Westminster will "tame" these would-be extremists, as the old Independent Labour Party members of Parliament had their Socialist ardour cooled.

12. This is assumed already to have happened by S. E. Finer in *Adversary Politics and Electoral Reform* (London: Clive Wigram, 1975). The evidence of this book shows

this is not the case. The examples given in the next paragraph, which would substantiate the Finer thesis, are hypothetical.

13. In 1945–51, the direction of domestic policy was very much dictated by Labour initiatives. It was consensual because the Conservative opposition did not wish to be identified with opposing proposals that it (rightly) believed might be popular. For an example of the Conservatives' willingness to move towards Labour positions, see *The Campaign Guide: General Election 1950* (London: Conservative Central Office, 1949).

14. "Callaghan bid to head off split," *The Guardian*, 20 September 1979.

15. Ian Waller, "After the Honeymoon," *Sunday Telegraph*, 14 October 1979.

16. "Waiting for Something to U-turn up," *The Economist*, 15 December 1979.

17. See, for example, the criticisms in Coates, ed. *What Went Wrong?* or the speech by the party chairman, Frank Allaun, in the 1979 *Labour Party Annual Conference Report* (London: Labour Party), and many speeches from the floor.

18. See, e.g., David Marquand, "Inquest on a Movement," *Encounter*, July 1979, pp. 8–18; Roy Jenkins, "Home Thoughts from Abroad"; and Peter Jenkins, "Staggering towards a Socialist Future," *The Guardian*, 21 October 1979. Note the ready admission by active Labour politicians of the need to reform the party — but not as the 1979 conference recommended — and the criticisms by ex-Labour ex-ministers of where their former party had been heading even before that Conference.

Index